Is Voting for Young People?

In 2008, everyone expected young people to turn out to vote in record numbers for the first youthful, hip, new media-savvy, African-American presidential candidate in history. They didn't. When Obama ran for reelection, he targeted young voters and they still didn't come to the polls in overwhelming numbers. What will happen in 2016, another potential history-making election?

Is Voting for Young People? explores the reasons why young people are less likely to follow politics and vote in the United States (as well as in many other established democracies) no matter who the candidates are, whether they tweet or blog, or what the issues may be. This brief, accessible, and provocative book suggests ways of changing that, and now includes a new chapter on young people's role in the 2008, 2012, and 2014 elections, looking ahead to 2016.

MARTIN P. WATTENBERG is Professor of Political Science at the University of California, Irvine, USA.

Is Voting for Young People?

With a New Elections Chapter for 2016

Fourth Edition

Martin P. Wattenberg
University of California, Irvine

Fourth edition published 2016
by Routledge
711 Third Avenue, New York, NY 10017

and by Routledge
2 Park Square, Milton Park, Abingdon, Oxon OX14 4RN

*Routledge is an imprint of the Taylor & Francis Group,
an informa business*

Third edition published 2012 by Pearson Education, Inc.
Second edition published 2008 by Pearson Education, Inc.
First edition published 2007 by Pearson Education, Inc.

Library of Congress Cataloging in Publication Data
Wattenberg, Martin P.,
   Is voting for young people / Martin P. Wattenberg.—Fourth
edition.
      pages cm.
   1. Young adults—Political activity. 2. Voting age.
3. Political participation. 4. Political culture. I. Title.
   HQ799.2.P6W38 2015
   324.6084'2—dc23
      2015028276

ISBN: 978-1-138-96239-2 (hbk)
ISBN: 978-1-138-96240-8 (pbk)
ISBN: 978-1-315-65945-9 (ebk)

Typeset in Times New Roman
by Sunrise Setting Ltd, Paignton, UK

For Mary and Elizabeth

Contents

CHAPTER 9

What Can Be Done? *page 198*

❖

Preface to the Fourth Edition

As this edition goes to press, one of the keys to understanding the 2016 elections will be the question of how many young people will turn out to vote. Given the current Democratic leanings of young Americans, a relatively good turnout will be good news for the Democratic nominee, whereas a disappointing turnout could spell trouble for the Democrats' chances of retaining the White House. Yet, even an increase in turnout from 2012 will probably be nothing to brag about. Unless the age patterns of electoral participation change dramatically in 2016, we can definitely expect Americans under the age of 30 to have the lowest turnout rate. As argued in Chapter 8, which expands on the original analysis of this book with data from the Obama era, last place in electoral participation is nothing to crow about.

Even in the age of Obama, the crux of the problem in getting young Americans involved in politics remains unchanged since this book was first published in 2006—namely, simply getting many young people to follow politics.

During the 2008 primaries, Michelle Obama famously promised a crowd at UCLA that "Barack will never allow you to go back to your lives as usual, uninvolved, uninformed." Some observers thought Mrs. Obama erred by assuming that many young people were politically apathetic; others viewed her statement as naïve, reflecting an insufficient appreciation of how difficult it is to motivate people who aren't interested in politics. This book demonstrates that the problem of youth apathy that Michelle Obama pointed to is indeed real. However, contrary to her confidence that it could be easily overcome by an inspirational leader, it also sheds light on how difficult it will be to substantially increase young people's political involvement. Young people have consistently given President Obama higher approval ratings than any other age group. But they have also regularly displayed very low levels of political attention throughout the Obama presidency. For example, the 2014 General Social Survey found that 63 percent of respondents under the age of 30 said that they were not interested in politics compared to just 29 percent of senior citizens. By contrast, in 1972 young people were actually more likely than the elderly to report high levels of political attention. This book lays out an argument as to why young people have been tuning out of politics in recent years, in the United States as well as in other established democracies.

Acknowledgments

This book relies on the cooperation of literally millions of survey respondents over the last six decades. In this era when survey response rates are declining, it bears remembering that so much scholarly research depends on the willingness of randomly chosen individuals to freely give a bit of their time. In addition to these anonymous individuals, I am grateful to the many scholars who have carried out these studies and generously made them available for others to analyze.

As this project evolved, numerous colleagues provided helpful comments and assistance in gathering data. I wish to especially thank Matthew Beckmann, Russell Dalton, George Edwards, David Farrell, Mark Gray, Hans-Dieter Klingemann, Arend Lijphart, Ian McAllister, Dieter Ohr, Thomas E. Patterson, Andrew Russell, Aiji Tanaka, Carole Uhlaner, and Jack Vowles. Students in my classes at the University of California, Irvine, and the University of New South Wales listened to my ideas on this subject and often helped me to see things from the perspective of their generation.

The original manuscript for this book and subsequent editions benefited from a thorough reading by the following reviewers: Robert Jackson of Florida State University; Martin Johnson of the University of California, Riverside; Miki Kittilson of Arizona State University; Brad Lockerbie of the University of Georgia; Sean Matheson of Knox College; Richard Niemi of the University of Rochester; and Jeffrey Stonecash of Syracuse University. Their helpful comments and suggestions resulted in many substantial improvements in this work. Together, they have improved the writing throughout and caught numerous oversights and errors. Any errors that may have made it into print are surely my responsibility.

I wish to thank all my editors for their hard work on the four editions of this book. Eric Stano, Donna Garnier, and Reid Hester steered the first three editions through smoothly at Pearson. Jennifer Knerr made the transition to Routledge for this edition a true pleasure and provided the inspiration for the thought-provoking little blurbs that now appear at the outset of every chapter.

Introduction

"You were more likely to see Bigfoot than a 20-year-old at the polls during the city's special election last Tuesday," read a newspaper article in May 2015. The story pointed out that according to official records just 333 residents between the ages of 18 and 24 voted in the election as compared to 5,084 voters who were 65 years of age or more.

Source: Adrian Glass-Moore, "Young voters missed last week's special election," *INFORUM*, May 4, 2015 (http://www.inforum.com/news/legislature/3737575-young-voters-missed-last-weeks-special-election, accessed October 1, 2015)

"Voting is for Old People," proclaimed a T-shirt printed and distributed by Urban Outfitters, a popular American clothing company. At Harvard's Kennedy School of Government, the perceived message of the shirt hit a raw nerve. Its director issued a public statement criticizing the slogan, saying that it could not be further from the truth—that voting is for everyone. In response, Urban Outfitters said they never intended to discourage anyone from voting. Rather, they asserted that their goal was to draw attention to the relative lack of participation of young adults in politics, a problem that many analysts and politicians acknowledge but few seem to be genuinely concerned about. As the clothing company said in a press release, the slogan "Voting is for Old People" was intended "to draw attention to the growing rift between politicians and their platforms and the concerns of young people in this country."[1] Having at least succeeded in drawing attention to their product line, Urban Outfitters soon discontinued the controversial T-shirt, letting the political issue quietly subside.

The central argument of this book is that over the last four decades, politics and voting have indeed become more and more the province of the elderly, which will be shown to be the case not only in the United States but also *throughout the world's advanced industrialized democracies.* There is in fact a rift between politicians and young adults, although not one of mutual contempt but rather of mutual neglect. Many young people don't vote simply because they don't follow politics. Moreover, because so many young people don't follow politics and don't vote, parties and politicians frequently don't bother with young people, thereby further widening the age bias in electoral participation.

All too often, low turnout rates among the young are considered to be a natural part of political life, and hence not worth fretting about. Scholars often write of a life-cycle pattern in which people become more aware of the political world as they age, and hence are more likely to vote. As such, it is often thought that today's young nonvoters will eventually show up at the polls and have their voices heard. If such a life cycle truly exists, it ought to be consistently found in 1) different eras and 2) across a wide range of democracies. The data examined in this book from a number of countries in the 1970s contradict the life-cycle hypothesis. Therefore, the pattern of young people being substantially less likely to follow politics regularly and to vote is a relatively new phenomenon that cries out for an explanation.

The fact that political apathy among young people is now so widespread across the world's established democracies makes it improbable that country-specific factors are at the root of the problem. Americans can reasonably speculate that a series of scandals from Watergate to Benghazi have turned off successive generations of young adults, Canadians can look to the twin problems of Quebec separatism and Western alienation, the Japanese can perhaps blame the long downturn in their country's economy, Germans can argue that dislocations from the unification process have led young people to turn away from politics, and the list goes on. But these are idiosyncratic reasons for a trend that is widely generalizable. Are we to conclude that it just so happens that various events in most of the world's established democracies have led young people to stay out of politics? When similar changes occur in country after country, we need to search for factors that are reshaping the political environment everywhere.

Communications technology is one such aspect of political life that has undergone transformation throughout the world's advanced industrialized societies—the United States, Western Europe, Japan, Canada, Australia, and New Zealand—in recent years. This book argues that changes in media habits from generation to generation have led to a new situation in which young people are far less likely to be exposed to news about public affairs than their elders. Young adults have not consciously decided to avoid political news in recent years; rather, having been socialized in a markedly different communications environment, they just have not picked up the same media habits that their parents and grandparents did. These media habits, which older people developed long ago in a different world, continue to serve them well in today's political environment—making them substantially more likely to follow politics and become familiar with the issues of the day. And the more one learns about public affairs and follows current events, the more one is likely to realize the stakes involved at the polls.

Because political apathy among young adults stems from their being tuned out from political news, the problem will be particularly difficult to reverse. Even if politicians pay special attention to young adults, it will be difficult for politicians to get through to this generation that pays so little attention to political news. But in actuality, there is very little incentive for politicians to appeal to young adults. Why should they pay any attention to young people if it is so well known that they do not follow political events or vote? Even young adults in the United States seem to be aware of this pattern. A nationwide study of 18- to 24-year-olds conducted by the Center for Information and Research on Civic Learning and Engagement in June 2002 found that 22 percent agreed with the statement that "Most young adults vote." At the same time, 74 percent agreed that "Voting is something older people do." And the consequences of this generation gap in voting were crystal clear to many of these young respondents: 68 percent agreed with the statement that "Politicians care more about the votes of older people than about me." These widely shared sentiments among America's young adults are all essentially correct. This book attempts to establish why these patterns have developed, both in the United States and in many other established democracies.

AN OVERVIEW

The first part of this book focuses on the root causes of the generation gap in voter turnout—changes in media consumption habits over time. Chapter 1 examines trends in newspaper reading, demonstrating that over the past three decades, each new cohort of young adults entering the electorate has been less and less likely to have developed the habit of perusing a daily newspaper. This trend is of particular significance because newspapers are by far the best source for learning about politics. Of course, one can learn about politics from other media sources such as television news. But by and large, television is merely a headline delivery service when it comes to politics. Furthermore, Chapter 2 demonstrates that over the past several decades, TV news has become a medium that appeals primarily to older people. When a few networks controlled the airwaves in the broadcasting era, political shows were hard to avoid and reached the young and old alike. In contrast, in the recent era of narrowcasting, young adults have grown up with remote controls in their hands and a plethora of alternatives to politics. Recent data from throughout the established democratic world indicate that when politics is on, young adults are off somewhere else.

With these changes in generational patterns of newspaper reading and TV news watching, the relationship between age and awareness of political events has been dramatically altered. A common saying among young people involved in politics once was that one should never trust anyone over 30. Now, as discussed in Chapter 3, when it comes to current political events and the governmental process, one could well say, "Don't ask anyone under 30," for chances are that they will not be informed. People know what they follow, and politics has unfortunately become a topic that the elderly follow much more closely than do young people. The result is that today's young adults are the least politically knowledgeable generation ever in the history of survey research.

With recent generations establishing modern lows for newspaper reading, TV news watching, and knowledge of public affairs, a significant generation gap has emerged in terms of voter participation in many established democracies. Chapter 4 outlines how getting young adults to vote in presidential and parliamentary elections has become more and more of a problem in the United States and elsewhere. This chapter also examines elections of lesser importance, where the age gap in terms of electoral participation has reached alarming levels in many countries. Chapter 5 then examines generational differences with regard to attitudes about civic duty. These data may well provide a window into the likely future of electoral participation. Because the current generation of young people is relatively unlikely to see voting as an important civic responsibility, many of them may well be lost as voters for the rest of their lives.

By passing up opportunities to vote, young adults are ceding important decisions to those who have different values and interests. Chapter 6 demonstrates that the concerns of young adults differ substantially from those of their elders, with generational differences clearly evident on Left–Right positioning as well as on various policy issues. In the United States and other established democracies, survey evidence from recent elections shows that more young people voting definitely would make a difference because the youth vote often favors different candidates and parties.

Some scholars have recently argued that young people make up for their low turnout rates through other means of participation in public life, such as volunteering or boycotting products. Chapter 7 evaluates this argument, finding that the overall outlook for the political participation of young people is not as bad as is the case with voting. Nevertheless, it is hardly a rosy scenario that could counterbalance their low electoral participation.

Some observers have also argued that the Obama campaign of 2008 inspired so many young people to get involved in politics that the age of youth apathy is now a remnant of the past. New to this 2016 edition, Chapter 8 examines young people's participation between 2008 and 2014. It finds that the problem of youth apathy was by no means solved in 2008, as turnout among young people only increased among racial minorities and quickly dissipated in 2012. Furthermore, young people sat out the midterm elections of the Obama presidency at alarming rates, with their turnout rates falling to rock-bottom single-digit percentages in some places in 2014.

Finally, Chapter 9 discusses a variety of reforms that could help ensure that voting is for young people just as much as it is for other age groups. Many good ideas have been proposed that probably would do some good. However, only the institution of compulsory election attendance has proved to be a cure-all for the problem of unequal political participation. Granted, many people may see this as an authoritarian step. Yet, it has worked very successfully in a number of countries, such as Australia, Belgium, and Greece. Given the typical requirements of citizenship such as paying taxes, reporting for jury duty, and registering for potential military service, requiring occasional participation in elections seems to be a relatively small imposition to achieve generational equality at the polls.

CHAPTER 1

The Aging of Regular Newspaper Readers

In 2014, the General Social Survey found that just 2 percent of people under the age of 25 reported reading a newspaper every day, whereas 47 percent never read a newspaper. Among senior citizens, 44 percent said they read a newspaper daily and just 18 percent said they never read a newspaper.

Go any place where a variety of people are waiting around in the morning, such as an airport terminal or a train station, and you are likely to observe a now-common behavior pattern: the younger someone is, the less likely he or she is reading a newspaper. It was not always this way. Old movie scenes portray everyone reading newspapers. Young and old alike are shown reading newspapers, as that was how most people got their news. Ever since the 1960s, however, when television supplanted newspapers as the major source of news information, the newspaper business has been fading.

The decline of newspaper consumption has almost completely been due to generational replacement, with each new cohort of young people less likely than its elders to read newspapers. There is little indication of people giving up on newspapers and canceling their subscriptions. Reading a newspaper every day is a habit that, once acquired, is generally continued throughout one's lifetime, and for most people such a routine either is or is not developed by the time a person reaches voting age. What has happened in recent years is that relatively few young adults have picked up this habit.

As with all the major trends outlined in this book, this is not just an American phenomenon. Throughout the established democracies, survey data over time show that regular newspaper readers are now considerably older than was the case in the 1970s. In country after country, the last three decades have seen a transformation of the newspaper from a medium for everyone to an information source primarily for older people.

This worldwide trend would be of little consequence were newspapers being replaced by another source of political information that people could learn as much from. But to date, no viable replacement for newspapers has emerged. One can, of course, learn the basic outline of current events from sources such as CNN's Headline News. But this channel is aptly named, as it covers only what a newspaper reader would get by simply scanning the headlines. If one really wants to be informed about political matters, decades of academic research support the conclusion that newspapers are the best media source.[2]

Over two centuries ago, James Madison foresaw not only the promise of American democracy but also how the then-young medium of newspapers could play a key role in enabling ordinary citizens to participate effectively in democratic governance. As Colleen Sheehan writes, "Madison envisioned newspapers serving as vehicles for circulation of the ideas of the literati to the people of the extensive American republic, resulting in the refinement and enlargement of the public views and the emergence of an enlightened public opinion."[3] Madison would probably be very pleased with the depth of content available in today's newspapers but disappointed that so many citizens are passing up the opportunity to avail themselves of this wealth of information.

Almost exactly 200 years after Madison assumed the presidency of the United States, his successor looked upon newspapers with indifference. In a fall 2003 interview with Brit Hume of *FOX News*, President George W. Bush clearly stated that he didn't read newspapers.[4] This statement led many pundits and scholars to gasp in amazement that a president could ignore such a valuable source of news about the world. Longtime White House correspondent Helen Thomas argued that Bush could hardly claim to be in touch with public opinion if he wasn't reading a newspaper. She wrote that "Anyone who wants to stay in touch with national, international and local events looks forward to reading the newspaper every day. The variety and breadth of newspaper stories make Americans the best-informed people in the world."[5] It should be noted that President Bush maintained that he did not need to read newspapers because his chief of staff and national security advisor provided him with daily news briefings. But this satisfied few critics, who wondered whether even the most trusted aides could be expected to relay a comprehensive sense of the news of the day to the commander in chief.

Left unsaid in this hullabaloo was the hard truth that the percentage of the American public who reads a daily newspaper has been declining for quite some time. Whether Bush's avoidance of newspapers is a good practice for a president or not, the fact that such a large proportion of the population no longer bothers to read a newspaper has made it easier for a president to say he doesn't either. A few decades ago, it probably would have seemed outlandish for the leader of the free world to say this; today, given the decline of newspapers, it is not. This chapter tells the story of how generational change has contributed to this transformation in the United States, as well as in most advanced industrialized democracies.

Who Reads a Newspaper Every Day Anymore?

This chapter's data presentation is premised on the theoretical perspective that newspaper reading is a well-ingrained habit. Data from the 1992–1996 American National Election Panel Study offer strong confirmation for this premise. In both years, the same randomly selected individuals were asked how many days they had read a newspaper in the past week. Sixty-seven percent of respondents who in 1992 had said they read a paper every day said the same thing four years later. In contrast, only 13 percent of the respondents who had said they had not read a paper every day during the past week in 1992 indicated they did so when they were reinterviewed in 1996. The correlation between the actual number of days a respondent said he or she read a newspaper in the past week in 1992 and in 1996 was quite impressive at .64. The stability coefficient for party identification, which is widely regarded as the most stable of all political attitudes, is typically about .80 over four years. Given the disruptions of people's routines that can easily occur in any given week, the fact that responses to the newspaper reading question are nearly as stable as party identification is solid evidence of a deep-rooted habit.

The most straightforward way to present data on newspaper reading routines is to report the percentage who say they read a paper every day of the week. Of course, most people who do not read a paper every day will occasionally pick one up and skim through it. In all likelihood, President Bush sometimes read a newspaper; when he said he didn't, he probably meant that it wasn't a habit for him. And it is the trends in this habit that we are interested in.

Table 1.1 displays survey data from 1957 to 2004 regarding the percentage of the adult American public who reported reading a newspaper every day of the week. In the late 1950s, surveys indicated that roughly three-quarters of the adult population (then defined as over 21 years of age) read a paper every day. Not shown in the data in Table 1.1 is the fact that this survey asked people how many papers they read as well as how often. Amazingly, 21 percent said they read two papers daily, and another 4 percent said they read three papers every day. Most of these people who read more than one paper a day were probably reading a morning and an afternoon paper. In the absence of the ability to turn on the TV in the evening to get the news, getting a paper that was published in the late afternoon was a good way to keep abreast of late-breaking events. As late as 1970, afternoon papers accounted for 58 percent of daily newspapers sold; by 2001, this figure had fallen to a mere 16 percent.[6]

The survey data show that in the 15 years between 1957 and 1972, there was only a slight decline in daily newspaper reading, though probably far fewer people were reading more than one newspaper a day by the early 1970s. Since the early 1970s, though, the decline in daily newspaper reading has been precipitous. In the 32 years from 1972 to 2004, this habit declined at the rate of approximately 1 percent a year. Should this trend continue

TABLE 1.1

Percent Reading a Newspaper Every Day of the Week, 1957–2004

1957	76
1958	75
1967	73
1972	69
1975	67
1977	63
1978	58
1982	53
1983	56
1985	53
1986	54
1987	56
1988	51
1989	50
1990	53
1991	52
1993	47
1994	50
1996	42
1998	43
2000	37
2002	42
2004	41

Sources: 1957 News Media Study; 1958 Omnibus Survey of Consumer Attitudes and Behavior; 1967 Political Participation in America Study; 1972–2004 General Social Surveys.

unabated, no one by the year 2045 will be reading a newspaper every day. Of course, such long-term projections can hardly be taken seriously given all the unforeseen factors that might intervene to accelerate or reverse the trend over the next 40 years. But people in the newspaper business are clearly concerned that they are losing customers at a significant and steady rate.[7] Even more alarming for them is the fact that young adults are not reading newspapers at nearly the same rate as previous generations, thereby making it likely that this trend will continue for decades to come.

The generational nature of the decline of daily newspaper reading is dramatically shown in the cohort data displayed in Table 1.2. Looking across the rows, one sees a good deal of stability within each cohort in terms of the percentage reading a newspaper every day. For example, of people born in my cohort (1953–1957), 42 percent in the mid-1970s said they read a newspaper every day, 43 percent in the late 1980s said they did so, and 38 percent in the 2000–2004 period said they did so. This compares poorly to the steady 75 percent rate of daily newspaper reading among my parents' cohort. Such a generational difference is hardly unusual; Table 1.2 clearly shows that since the beginning of the TV age, new cohorts have been less likely to report reading a newspaper every day. Thus, the routine of reading a newspaper every day is not evident at nearly the same rate among new cohorts as compared to the age groups that are currently dying out. At present, seven out of ten of the most elderly adults have read a newspaper every day throughout their lives. In contrast, among the young adults who are replacing them in the electorate, only about two in ten have thus far developed this media consumption habit.

TABLE 1.2
Cohort Analysis of Percent Reading a Newspaper Every Day

BORN IN:	2000–2004	1987–1989	1972–1977	1967	1957
1978–1982	20				
1973–1977	19				
1968–1972	26	22			
1963–1967	31	30			
1958–1962	33	37			
1953–1957	38	43	42		
1948–1952	46	53	50		
1943–1947	50	58	56	57	
1938–1942	55	57	65	64	
1933–1937	62	65	72	75	70*
1928–1932	72	66	74	79	74
1923–1927		74	79	75	78
1918–1922		74	79	79	76
1913–1917		72	79	77	82
1908–1912			78	79	80
1903–1907			79	76	82
1898–1902			77	78	77
1893–1897				75	75

*Only 1933 to 1936 here.

Sources: 1957 News Media Study; 1967 Political Participation in America Study; 1972–2004 General Social Surveys.

HAS READING A NEWSPAPER FOR POLITICAL CONTENT CHANGED?

Newspapers are an incredibly diverse source of information on all sorts of topics—politics, sports, weather, business, culture, health, etc. Therefore, it cannot be assumed that people who read a newspaper every day are actually taking in the political news. They may well subscribe to a daily newspaper in order to check out one or two sections of the newspaper that have nothing to do with politics. In the era before television news, it may well have been the case that young people picked up a newspaper only because it was the primary means for checking the weather and sports scores. Fortunately, the Survey Research Center's 1957 and 1958 media usage surveys asked about the types of newspaper stories people usually read. Table 1.3 presents the data by age group from these late-1950s surveys regarding reading stories about national politics. Respondents who were under 30 years old were somewhat less likely than other age groups to say that they read all the way through the national political news. On the other hand, seniors were a bit more likely to report that they never read a newspaper at all. Overall, the correlation between age and level of attention to political stories in the newspaper was a mere .03. In sum, young,

TABLE 1.3
Frequency of Reading About National Politics by Age, 1957–1958 (in percents)

	READ ALL	READ SOME	GLANCE AT	SKIP OVER	NEVER READ THE PAPER
21–29	16	37	20	18	9
30–44	24	37	18	14	7
45–64	22	38	16	15	9
65+	27	30	12	17	14

Question wording: "How often do you read the newspapers?" (If at all), "Of course, all people aren't interested in the same things in the paper, so I would like to get an idea of the kinds of things that interest you in the paper. Would you tell me about how often you usually read each kind of news—do you read it all the way through, read some of it, just glance at it, or skip over it?" How about "stories about national politics"?

Source: Combined data from 1957 U.S. Media Study and Spring 1958 U.S. Survey of Consumer Attitudes and Behavior.

TABLE 1.4
Percent Reading Newspapers About the Campaign by Age, 1960–2004

	18–29	30–44	45–64	65+	DIFFERENCE BETWEEN 65+ AND <30
1960	84	80	81	74	+10
1964	75	80	80	77	−2
1968	68	81	76	72	−4
1972	49	59	62	61	−11
1976	68	78	77	70	−2
1980	56	78	76	72	−16
1984	62	77	77	70	−8
1988	35	47	57	57	−22
1992	35	50	57	60	−25
1996	28	39	52	60	−32
2000	27	35	48	56	−29
2004	34	39	51	61	−27

Question wording: 1952–1976: "We're interested in this interview in finding out whether people paid much attention to the election campaign this year. Take newspapers for instance—did you read about the campaign in any newspaper?"; 1980–1984: "Did you read about the campaign in any newspapers?"; 1988–2004: "How many days in the past week did you read a daily newspaper?" (If R has read a daily newspaper in the past week:) "Did you read about the campaign in any newspaper?"

Source: American National Election Studies.

middle aged, and old alike took in newspaper coverage of national politics at about the same rate.

Unfortunately, there are no recent survey data specifically on newspaper consumption of national political stories. The best available time-series data are from the American National Election Studies (ANES), which have continually asked respondents whether they read about the presidential campaign in the newspaper or not. Table 1.4 presents these data by age group for the period from 1960 to 2004. From 1960 to 1976, there was no consistent difference in this measure between the youngest and oldest citizens. Since 1980, though, those under 30 have been substantially less likely to pick up a newspaper and read about the presidential race. In both 1996 and 2000, senior citizens were more than twice as likely to say that they had read campaign articles in newspapers compared to people under 30. The ANES data clearly confirm that not only is newspaper readership down sharply among young adults but also that today's youth are much less likely to follow politics in the newspaper than their parents and grandparents were at the same age.

CAN SIMILAR PATTERNS BE FOUND IN OTHER ESTABLISHED DEMOCRACIES?

If competition from television is the principal reason why younger Americans have not gotten into the newspaper reading habit, then similar generational patterns should be found throughout much of the world. Even tiny, isolated Bhutan now has television service, and as a result has seen its way of life transformed.[8] If television has had that sort of effect in Bhutan, then it is a fairly safe assumption that other advanced industrialized democracies like the United States will have experienced similar effects. On the other hand, if newspapers continue to appeal to young people in other countries, then the American pattern must stem from something particular about the quality or appeal of American newspapers, or the nature of American politics.

In order to assess whether other countries have experienced the same generational patterns as the United States, one needs cross-national data on the regularity of newspaper reading in many countries from different eras. Various data exist for a number of countries, but for the sake of comparability it is best to look to collaborative studies that have asked identically worded questions at roughly the same time in a wide range of countries. The earliest data I could find in a cross-national study was the 1981–1983 World Values Study, which asked respondents throughout much of the world whether they regularly read a daily newspaper. Table 1.5 displays the results from this question by age category in the United States and 12 other established democracies. These results show that as of the early 1980s, the correlation between age and regular newspaper reading in the United States was roughly in line with what was found in other democracies. In 10 of the 13 countries,

TABLE 1.5

Percent Who Regularly Read a Newspaper by Age
in 13 Countries in the Early 1980s

	18–29	30–44	45–64	65+	DIFFERENCE BETWEEN 65+ AND 18–29	CORRELATION WITH AGE
FRANCE	34	42	60	69	+35	.25
GERMANY	72	84	89	86	+14	.17
USA	61	70	78	75	+14	.12
CANADA	59	68	70	72	+13	.09
NETHERLANDS	82	88	93	90	+8	.10
UK	76	80	91	83	+7	.10
DENMARK	82	87	90	88	+6	.07
SWEDEN	90	96	98	96	+6	.07
JAPAN	75	89	88	79	+4	.07
BELGIUM	55	61	62	59	+4	.05
NORWAY	92	95	99	94	+2	.08
IRELAND	78	80	75	66	–12	–.08
ITALY	47	58	44	32	–15	–.09

Question wording: "Do you regularly read a daily newspaper? That is, at least 4 out of every 6 issues?"

Source: 1981–1983 World Values Study.

there was only slight evidence of younger people being less likely to read newspapers frequently. The three exceptions were France, where young people were much less likely to read a paper, and Ireland and Italy, where senior citizens were actually the least likely to be habitual newspaper consumers.

For a current-day comparison, the best available data in a cross-national study can be found in the 2002–3 European Social Survey, which asked respondents how much time they spent reading a paper on an average weekday. As shown in Table 1.6, the relationship between age and frequency of newspaper reading was much higher in these recent survey data. Of the countries covered by the recent European Social Survey, nine were also included in the World Values Study of the early 1980s. On average, senior citizens in these countries were 10 percent less likely to classify themselves as regular newspaper readers in recent surveys than in the early 1980s. In contrast, respondents under 30 years of age were 38 percent less likely to meet the criteria for regular newspaper readership in the 2002–2003 period than young people in the same countries had been two decades earlier. The result is a clear increase in the relationship between age and frequent newspaper reading in every country for which data are available over the past two decades.

Germany provides an especially clear example of this phenomenon. In both Tables 1.5 and 1.6, Germany ranks second in terms of the relationship between age and newspaper reading. In the early 1980s, though, there was only a slight tendency for younger Germans to be less likely to read newspapers—72 percent of Germans under 30 said they regularly read a newspaper compared to between 84 and 89 percent among the other age categories. By 2002, one can see a strong linear pattern in the German survey data, with only 28 percent of Germans under 30 reporting that

TABLE 1.6

Percent of Europeans Who Read a Newspaper for at Least 30 Minutes on a Typical Weekday in 2002–2003

	18–29	30–44	45–64	65+	DIFFERENCE BETWEEN 65+ AND 18–29	CORRELATION WITH AGE*
DENMARK	18	29	52	72	+54	.42
GERMANY	28	37	58	74	+46	.34
SWEDEN	37	42	65	80	+43	.36
FINLAND	39	46	63	80	+41	.36
SWITZERLAND	35	44	60	75	+40	.31
NETHERLANDS	39	40	64	75	+36	.33
NORWAY	50	58	78	86	+36	.32
FRANCE	21	24	37	51	+30	.20
BELGIUM	26	30	38	54	+28	.22
AUSTRIA	37	43	54	65	+28	.21
UK	43	40	52	65	+23	.22
IRELAND	48	50	66	70	+22	.15
ITALY	30	35	37	32	+2	.03

Question wording: "On an average weekday, how much time, in total, do you spend reading the newspapers?"

*For the correlations, responses to the newspaper question are recoded into approximate number of minutes as follows: no time at all = 0; less than ½ hour = 15; ½ hour to 1 hour = 45; more than 1 hour, up to 1½ hours = 75; more than 1½ hours, up to 2 hours = 105; more than 2 hours, up to 2½ hours = 135; more than 2½ hours, up to 3 hours = 165; more than 3 hours = 195.

Source: European Social Survey, 2002–3.

they read a paper for at least 30 minutes a day compared to 74 percent among German senior citizens.

Ireland presents another good example. Like Germany, Ireland's rank in terms of the correlation between age and reading a paper on a regular basis was the same at both time points, being relatively weak in both tables. In the early 1980s, the only substantial difference in newspaper reading habits by age in Ireland was that senior citizens were actually the least likely to be regular readers. Two decades later, however, senior citizens were clearly the most likely to read newspapers, with 70 percent saying they spent at least 30 minutes with one on a typical day compared to just 48 percent among young adults.

Cross-national data with regard to reading newspapers specifically for political news also show clear evidence of the aging of the newspaper audience. The World Values Study did not ask such a question, but fortunately this is available for eight nations in the 1973–1976 Political Action study. Table 1.7 presents by age category the percentage in each country who

TABLE 1.7
Percent Who Read About Politics in the Newspaper Often or Sometimes in Eight Countries, 1973–1976

	18–29	30–44	45–64	65+	DIFFERENCE BETWEEN 65+ AND 18–29	CORRELATION WITH AGE*
NETHERLANDS	58	70	65	71	+13	.07
USA	66	81	81	73	+7	.09
UK	62	68	70	67	+5	.09
SWITZERLAND	58	70	71	63	+5	.04
AUSTRIA	56	59	60	57	+1	.04
FINLAND	63	62	64	63	0	.04
GERMANY	72	76	75	67	–5	.00
ITALY	54	37	32	25	–29	–.23

Question wording: "How often do you read about politics in the newspapers: often, sometimes, seldom, or never?"

*Responses to the newspaper question were recoded as follows for the correlations: often = 100; sometimes = 67; seldom = 33; never = 0.

Source: Political Action: An Eight Nation Study, 1973–1976.

reported that they often or sometimes read about politics[9] in the newspapers, as well as correlations summarizing how closely these two variables were related. Both the correlations and the percentages indicate that in the mid-1970s, there was only a slight tendency in most of these countries for older people to read newspaper stories about politics more frequently than younger people did so. The exception is Italy, where young Italians of the 1970s—the only group not to have experienced any of the Mussolini era—were substantially more likely to be reading about politics in the newspapers.

Today, young people in all the established European democracies are significantly less prone to spend a fair amount of time reading about politics in the newspaper, as demonstrated by the data displayed in Table 1.8. All the European countries for which we can compare more recent patterns to those from the 1970s show a notable increase in the correlation between age and reading newspaper stories about public affairs. In the mid-1970s Political Action data (Table 1.7), this correlation averaged .01 in the seven European countries (or .05 if excluding Italy). In the more recent European Social Survey data, the relationship in these same countries had increased to an average of .20 (or .22 if excluding Italy).[10]

In sum, the evidence clearly supports the conclusion that the pattern of aging audiences reading political stories in newspapers is quite common throughout the world's established democracies. Newspapers have become more and more for the elderly. And if young citizens are to learn about politics, it seems that it will have to be from some other media. Young people throughout the world's advanced industrialized democracies have simply not gotten into the routine of picking up a daily newspaper and reading about current events.

TABLE 1.8
Percent of Europeans Who Read a Daily Newspaper at Least 30 Minutes to Learn About Politics in 2002–2003

	18–29	30–44	45–64	65+	DIFFERENCE BETWEEN 65+ AND <30	CORRELATION WITH AGE*
DENMARK	8	15	28	48	+40	.33
NORWAY	20	24	40	53	+33	.28
FINLAND	12	17	28	45	+33	.29
SWITZERLAND	11	17	29	41	+30	.23
NETHERLANDS	14	19	29	42	+28	.23
SWEDEN	11	13	26	36	+25	.25
GERMANY	10	13	23	35	+25	.24
IRELAND	20	24	41	44	+24	.17
UK	11	13	17	28	+17	.16
AUSTRIA	18	18	28	33	+15	.15
FRANCE	12	12	20	24	+12	.12
BELGIUM	11	11	18	22	+11	.11
ITALY	11	14	20	20	+9	.08

Question wording: "On an average weekday, how much time, in total, do you spend reading the newspapers? And how much of this time is spent reading about politics and current affairs?"

*For the correlations, responses to the newspaper question are recoded into approximate number of minutes as follows: no time at all = 0; less than ½ hour = 15; ½ hour to 1 hour = 45; more than 1 hour, up to 1½ hours = 75; more than 1½ hours, up to 2 hours = 105; more than 2 hours, up to 2½ hours = 135; more than 2½ hours, up to 3 hours = 165; more than 3 hours = 195.

Source: European Social Survey, 2002–2003.

Do Young Adults Just not like to Read?

One possible explanation for why recent generations have not gotten into the newspaper reading habit may be that they are simply less fond of reading. Growing up with TV, computers, and video games may have created a markedly different socialization process in which reading plays a significantly smaller role in their lives. If this is the case, then the age-related trends we have found for newspaper consumption might be seen as part of a general societal failure to instill an appreciation for reading in recent generations. Yet, although this seems to be a sensible hypothesis, the available survey evidence is not at all supportive of it.

Contrary to any notion that socialization has come to be less centered on books, the 2000 U.S. General Social Survey found that today's young adults grew up with more books around the house than previous generations. This survey asked respondents how many books there were around their homes when they were 16 years old. Two-thirds of respondents under the age of 30 said that there had been at least 50 books around their homes, compared to 56 percent among those between the ages of 30 and 64, and 36 percent among senior citizens. The greater availability of books during the socialization of younger people probably reflects the increase in American education levels over the years.

As the overall level of education has increased over the past half century, Americans have in fact become more likely to say that they read books. Fifty-seven percent of respondents interviewed in the 2002 national survey of Public Participation in the Arts said they had read a book in the past year compared to just 35 percent of respondents in the 1957 News Media Study. In both studies, young people were actually slightly more likely to report having read a book than older people, but in both cases the relationship between age and reading books was insignificant once education was controlled for.[11]

Data over time are not available from other countries, but recent surveys show that the current American pattern is typical. In August/September 2001, the Eurobarometer asked people in the European Economic Community whether they had read a book for reasons other than for work or school in the last year. The correlation between age and reading a book for pleasure ranged from −.13 in Italy to .05 in the United Kingdom, averaging a mere −.02 in the 11 established democracies where the question was asked. Similarly, in the 2000 Japanese Social Survey, the correlation between age and whether or not respondents said they usually read at least one book in a month was −.06. In sum, these slightly negative correlations indicate that young adults in established democracies are slightly more likely to read books than their elders. Today's young adults do in fact read—they just don't usually read newspapers.

Conclusion: A Future for Newspapers?

The financial viability of the printed newspaper being delivered to one's front door every morning is therefore surely in doubt. Many people believe that the future of the newspaper business lies with the Internet. Today, most major newspapers have an online edition. It is certainly conceivable that as a younger generation accustomed to receiving news electronically comes of age, the newspaper business will make a successful transition to an Internet-based medium. Available survey data from the United States and Europe do show that the younger someone is, the more likely he or she is to read newspaper articles online. But this pattern probably stems simply from younger people's greater computer literacy. There is little indication that reading newspapers online has yet become an important facet of the Internet experience for young people.

Indeed, the frequency with which even young adults go to newspaper websites has thus far been relatively unimpressive. A May 2004 Pew survey found that only 7 percent of respondents under 30 years old said that they regularly read "the websites of major national newspapers such as the *USA Today.com*, *New York Times.com*, or the *Wall Street Journal* online." Similarly, the 2012 Pew media survey found that only 7 percent of respondents under the age of 30 had read a newspaper online the previous day.

In Europe, the experience with newspaper websites has been relatively similar. The August/September 2001 Eurobarometer asked people what they usually used the Internet for, providing "reading articles on the websites of newspapers" as one possible response. Overall, just 8 percent of adult citizens in the European Economic Community said they usually did so; Europeans between the ages of 18 and 29 led the way, with 13 percent of them regularly reading newspapers online.

In sum, newspaper websites have a long way to go in order to reach anywhere near the number of young people that traditional newspapers have long managed to reach among older citizens. Today's young adults can potentially learn a tremendous amount about politics from newspaper websites, *if they so choose,* but it would appear that very few are choosing to do so.

One might ponder the findings of this chapter and conclude that although television will never provide as much detailed information as newspapers do, at least young adults can partially make up for their lack of interest in newspapers by watching TV news. However, as will be seen in the next chapter, when politics is on television, young people are more likely than ever to tune out.

CHAPTER 2

The Aging Audience for Politics on TV

In 2014, CNN also had the youngest audience in cable news, with a median age of 58, compared to 61 for MSNBC and 68 for Fox News.

> Source: Matt Wilstein, *Mediaite*, December 30, 2014 (http://www.mediaite.com/tv/2014-cable-news-ratings-cnn-beats-msnbc-in-primetime-demo-fox-still-1, accessed October 1, 2015)

It didn't take long after the start of television broadcasting for newspapers to realize the potential competition they were facing. In fact, one of the reasons *TV Guide* became a top-selling publication was that many newspapers would not print television schedules for fear of the competition from the new medium. By the late 1950s, astute politicians were realizing the potential of television. A year before he was elected president, John F. Kennedy wrote in an article for *TV Guide* about the impact TV was already having, arguing that "TV has altered drastically the nature of our political campaigns, conventions, constituents, candidates, and costs."[12]

The revolutionary effect of television on politics was evident to Hollywood early on as well. In the classic 1958 movie *The Last Hurrah*, Spencer Tracy's character urges his nephew to follow him on the campaign trail to witness a traditional political campaign while he still can. Tracy's lines go as follows:

> *It's my guess that the old-fashioned political campaign in a few years will be as extinct as the dodo. It will all be TV.... Mind you, I use the TV sometimes, but I also get out into the wards. I speak in arenas, armories, street corners, anywhere I can get a crowd. I even kiss babies.... But there's no use kidding myself—it is on the way out.*

While this prediction now seems prophetic, it also tells us just how clear it was to those who lived through the early years of television that politics was being rapidly transformed.

For political scientists, though, the impact of television on politics was long considered to be minimal. This conclusion was especially prevalent with regard to learning about political issues. For example, Patterson and McClure's classic study of the 1972 U.S. presidential election, aptly titled *The Unseeing Eye*, concluded that the networks "may have allowed Americans to 'see' the campaign, but in so doing they have added nothing of substance to the voters' civic education."[13] The widely acknowledged superficiality of television news coverage for quite some time led scholars to largely ignore the impact the medium was having on politics.

Another reason that so much early scholarship regarding television and politics fit under the rubric of "minimal effects" is that most of these studies were looking for direct impacts—for example, whether the media influenced how people voted.[14] When the focus turned to how the media affect *what Americans think about*, more impressive results were uncovered. In a series of controlled laboratory experiments, Shanto Iyengar and Donald Kinder subtly manipulated the stories that participants saw on the TV news.[15] They found that they could significantly affect the importance people attached to a given problem by splicing a few stories about it into the news over the course of a week. Iyengar and Kinder do not maintain that the networks can make something out of nothing or conceal problems that actually exist. But they do conclude that "what television news does, instead, is alter the priorities Americans attach to a circumscribed set of problems, all of which are plausible contenders for public concern."[16] Subsequent research by Miller and Krosnick has revealed that agenda-setting effects are particularly strong among politically knowledgeable citizens who trust the media. Thus, rather than television news manipulating the public, they argue that agenda setting reflects a deliberate and thoughtful process on the part of sophisticated citizens who rely on an information source they have come to trust.[17]

But who are these viewers whose receptiveness to the messages conveyed by TV news are the ones setting the public agenda? All too often, it is assumed that they are representative of the public at large because of the vast size of the audience reached by major broadcast networks. Such an assumption may well have been valid in the era when a few networks dominated the market in the United States and other established democracies. However, in today's world of a plethora of television channels, the representativeness of the TV news audience can no longer be taken for granted. As this chapter shows, the audience for TV news has become increasingly skewed toward the elderly in recent decades. When politics is on, young people are off somewhere else, or are reaching for the remote control. Moreover, as with the findings regarding newspapers, data over time show that such generational differences were not always the case.

Central to any generational phenomenon are changes in socialization experiences. Since the early 1980s, young people have been socialized in a rapidly changing media environment that has been radically different from that experienced by the past couple of generations. The first major American networks—ABC, NBC, and CBS—adopted the term "broadcasting" in the names of their companies because their signal was being sent out to a broad audience. When these networks dominated the industry, each had to deal with general topics that the public as a whole was concerned with, such as politics and government. However, with the development of cable and satellite TV, market segmentation has taken hold. Sports buffs can watch ESPN all day; music buffs can tune to MTV or VH1; history buffs can glue their dial to the History Channel; and so forth. Rather than appealing to a general audience, channels such as ESPN, MTV, and C-SPAN focus on a narrow, particular interest. Hence, their mission has often been termed "narrowcasting," rather than the traditional "broadcasting."

Because of the narrowcasting revolution, today's youth have grown up in an environment in which public affairs news has not been as readily visible as it was in the past. Major political events were once shared national experiences. However, the current generation of young adults is the first to grow up in a media environment in which there are few such shared experiences. As channels have proliferated, it has become much easier to avoid exposure to politics altogether by simply grabbing the remote control. It has become particularly difficult for political programming on television to get through to a generation who has channel surfed all their lives. This chapter tells the story of how young people have come to tune out politics on TV, both in the United States and in most established democracies.

Is Network TV News
a Dying Dinosaur?

For a time, the anchors of the three nightly news broadcasts were major figures in American political life. As Jeff Alan writes, "For all of us who grew up with the evening news anchors in our living rooms and family rooms five nights a week, it's fair to say that we saw more of the anchors than we saw of most of our neighbors, and even some of our close friends and relatives."[18] In 1974, the American National Election Study actually asked people to rate news anchors on a feeling thermometer scale ranging from 0 to 100, just as they did for major political leaders. Respondents were told that if they did not recognize a name, or felt they could not rate that individual, just to say so. All but 7 percent were able to rate Walter Cronkite of CBS, and all but 17 percent rated John Chancellor of NBC and Howard K. Smith of ABC. By comparison, 39 percent could not rate Senator Jackson, 52 percent could not rate Senator Mondale, and 65 percent could not rate Senator Bentsen—all of whom were prominent senators gearing up for a run at the presidency. By the end of 1980, one could make a legitimate argument that network newscasts had played a signifi-cant role in the political downfalls of Presidents Johnson, Nixon, and Carter due to the way the newscasts drew attention to those presidents' shortcomings. As Barbara Matusow wrote about the stars of the evening news in 1983, "They have taken their place beside presidents, congressmen, labor leaders, industrialists, and others who shape public policy and private attitudes."[19]

Over the last quarter century, however, the NBC, CBS, and ABC nightly news broadcasts have gone from being instrumental in setting the nation's agenda to the TV equivalent of dinosaurs on their last legs. During the 1968–1969 TV season, the combined audience of these three news programs on a typical evening was an incredible 50 percent of the American public. At about this time, Walter Cronkite was often called "the most trusted man in America." Thus, when Cronkite's view on the Vietnam War turned negative after the 1968 Tet Offensive, President Johnson quite reasonably concluded that if he had lost Cronkite's support, then he could no longer count on the support of the American people. Today, if a TV news anchor were to come out against the Afghanistan War, President Obama would hardly be likely to take much notice. None of today's news anchors enjoys anything approaching the audience share that Cronkite long enjoyed. As can be seen in the Nielsen ratings displayed in Table 2.1, the combined rating of the three network broadcasts steadily declined from 50 in 1968–1969 to just 20 in 2003–2004. As *New York Times* media critic Frank Rich wrote in 2002, "The No. 1 cliché among media critics is that we're watching the 'last hurrah' of network news anchors as we have known them for nearly half a century."[20]

It doesn't take much analytical ability these days to recognize that the network news broadcasts are barely hanging on, relying on older viewers who got into the habit of viewing these shows decades ago. Just as one can easily guess the demographics of people most likely to watch the Super Bowl by noting the many advertisements for beer and chips, so one can easily see that the network news audience is quite elderly by keeping an eye on the ads. For example, on one randomly chosen night (January 13, 2004), the *CBS Nightly News* was interspersed with commercials for the following products: Pepto Bismol, Ambien, Ex-Lax, Pepcid Complete, Imitrex, Ester-C, Dulcolax, Maalox, Wellbutrin XL, Detrol LA, and Benefiber. If one doesn't know what some of these products are, one is probably better off that way—suffice it to say

TABLE 2.1
The Decline in Ratings of U.S. National Network Evening News, 1980–2004

1968–1969*	50
(ALL-TIME HIGH)	
1980–1981	37
1981–1982	36
1982–1983	35
1983–1984	33
1984–1985	33
1985–1986	34
1986–1987	31
1987–1988	30
1988–1989	29
1989–1990	29
1990–1991	28
1991–1992	28
1992–1993	28
1993–1994	28
1994–1995	26
1995–1996	24
1996–1997	23
1997–1998	23
1998–1999	22
1999–2000	24
2000–2001	23
2001–2002	22
2002–2003	21
2003–2004	20

*The 1968–1969 ratings are inferred through the information provided in *The State of the News Media, 2005*, which shows that the three nightly newscasts saw their ratings decline by 59 percent from their peak in the 1968–1969 season.

Sources: 1980–1999: *Report on Television* (New York: Nielsen Media Research, 2000), p. 21; 1969 and 2000–2003: *The State of the News Media, 2005* (http://www.stateofthemedia.org/2005/index.asp) (accessed March 14, 2005).

that these ads are not for anything that one would buy for pleasure. Even products that could theoretically appeal to all age groups were advertised so as to appeal to senior citizens. An ad for dinner rolls from Pillsbury featured an elderly couple who raved about how the package allowed them to use only a few at a time, which was great now that their kids had moved out. Coricidon was portrayed not just as a cold remedy but also as a treatment appropriate for someone with high blood pressure. And Quaker Oatmeal was described as a good food to reduce cholesterol.

The generational nature of the decline of the network TV news is clearly shown in the cohort data from 1967, 1984, and 2004 displayed in Table 2.2. Overall, these surveys show that the percentage of the public who said they watched a network news broadcast every night was 72 percent in 1967, 45 percent in 1984, and 29 percent in 2004. This rate of decline almost perfectly parallels the trend found in the Nielsen ratings, thereby lending added confidence in the results of these surveys. Unlike the case with newspaper reading habits, the magnitude of this decline has been so great that it is apparent that over the years, some people within each cohort have gotten out of the routine of watching the network news every night. The fact that older people got into the habit of regularly watching these broadcasts during their heyday has left senior citizens as the primary audience for such shows today. In 1967, there was relatively little variation in news viewing habits by age, and TV news producers could hardly write off young adults, given that roughly two out of three said they had watched such broadcasts every night. In contrast, by 2004 senior citizens were four times more likely than those under 30 to say that they had watched the network news every night in the past week. Nielsen Media Research reported that the median age of viewers of the *CBS, ABC,* and *NBC News* from September 2003 through

TABLE 2.2

Cohort Analysis of Percent Watching U.S. Evening
Network TV News on a Daily Basis

BORN IN:	2004	1984	1967
1983–1986	8	–	–
1973–1982	15	–	–
1963–1972	21	24	–
1953–1962	28	28	–
1943–1952	42	35	64
1933–1942	47	51	68
1923–1932	52	62	69
1913–1922	–	67	73
1903–1912	–	70	76
1893–1902	–	–	79
1882–1892	–	–	79

Question wording: 1967: "How often do you watch the news broadcasts on TV—every day, a few times a week, about once a week, less than once a week, or never?"; 1984: "How often do you watch the national network news on TV—every day, 3 or 4 times a week, once or twice a week, or less often?"; 2004: "How many days in the past week did you watch the national network news on TV?"

Sources: 1967 Political Participation in America Study; 1984 and 2004 American National Election Studies.

early February 2004 was almost exactly 60 years of age—18 years older than the audience for a typical prime-time program.[21] Perhaps more than any other genre of programming, network news has become television for "old people."

A Pew Research Center survey from January 2004 casts further light on young adults' relative lack of reliance on broadcast news programs. Respondents were asked how often, if ever, they learned something about the presidential campaign or the candidates from a variety of media sources. Among respondents under 30 years old, 23 percent said they regularly learned something from network newscasts as compared to 21 percent from comedy TV shows. Commenting on this survey finding, Jon Stewart of the *Daily Show* at first dismissed out of hand any notion that young people were turning to his comedy show to learn about political events. Lately, his show has adopted the slogan of "Keeping America Informed— Unintentionally." If young Americans are putting such inadvertent learning from comedy shows on a par with what they get from the nightly network news, then clearly they are not getting much from the traditional NBC, CBS, and ABC broadcasts.

IS CABLE NEWS PICKING UP THE SLACK?

Of course, viewers now have an alternative to the 30-minute network news shows in the form of around the-clock news on CNN, MSNBC, and the FOX News Channel. The 24-hour format of cable news is especially well suited to the lifestyles of younger people, who are more likely to be constantly on the go with ever-changing schedules. Data from the 2004 Pew Research Center's media consumption study bear out this point. This survey asked a national sample the following question: "Are you more the kind of person who watches or listens to the news at regular times, or are you more the kind of person who checks in on the news from time to time?" Sixty-five percent of respondents under the age of 30 chose the latter option, compared to 45 percent among people between the ages of 30 and 64 and just 33 percent among senior citizens. Given how cable news is so compatible with young adults' flexible daily schedules, it should come as little surprise to find that the under-30 crowd is far more likely to say that they learn more about politics from these channels than from the broadcast networks.[22]

On the positive side, there can be little doubt that there is a good deal of *potential* for learning about politics from watching the seemingly endless supply of political coverage from cable news channels. This potential is nicely illustrated by one finding from the Pew Research Center's January 2004 study of political engagement and media usage. Among the 7 percent of respondents who scored highest on political engagement—those who said they followed the campaign closely, enjoyed following it, and were familiar with all the campaign events and facts that the survey asked about—cable news was the news source they most frequently relied upon for information about the campaign.[23] If one is truly motivated to follow all the ins and outs of political life, then around-the-clock cable news channels provide far more opportunities than ever before in the history of television.

Yet, it is important to note that the potential of cable news is often not realized in practice. Although these channels have seemingly unlimited opportunities to cover political events and issues, their resources are far from up to the task. Political scientist William Taubman experienced the constraints of cable news firsthand when he served as CNN's expert analyst during the Reagan–Gorbachev summit in 1988. Taubman "thought of the all-news network as having twenty-four hours a day to play with" and proposed numerous interviews with Soviet citizens about their country's struggle to transform itself. However, he soon found that CNN thought of itself as having "forty-eight half-hour segments, each of which had to cover the world and pay for that coverage with regularly scheduled features."[24] Of the numerous interviews he recommended, only a few were done, each lasting just a couple of minutes. And when Taubman was on the air, it usually wasn't long before he heard the dreaded words of "Wrap it up and head for commercial" in his earpiece.

William Taubman's experience is instructive as to the short-comings of cable news. A content analysis of CNN, FOX News, and MSNBC programming confirms just how little substantive information is usually conveyed via cable news channels. Columbia University's Project for Excellence in Journalism analyzed 240 hours of cable news programming during 2003. Their report on this content analysis provides a telling indictment of the medium. Among their many findings were that: 1) only 11 percent of the time was taken up with written and edited stories; 2) the role of the reporter was primarily to talk extemporaneously; 3) stories were repeated frequently, usually without any important new information; and 4) coverage of the news was spotty, ignoring many important topics. Network news may well still fit Patterson and McClure's description of "the unseeing eye," but the Columbia study is even less flattering to cable news, aptly labeling much of it as simply "talk radio on television."[25] As media critic Thomas Rosenstiel writes, "Network journalism originally was designed not to make a profit but to create prestige. Cable is all about profit and keeping costs low. What is disappearing is an idealism about the potential of TV as a medium to better our politics and society."[26]

In sum, more people—particularly young adults—may say that cable news is their primary source of political information, but there is good reason to be skeptical about how much the *typical* person with only limited political interest actually absorbs from these channels. The combined rating for the three-hour-long news shows on cable (*Newsnight* on CNN, *Special Report* on FOX News, and *Countdown* on MSNBC) was a minuscule 2.3 as of January 2005. Thus, the audience size of these programs was a mere tenth of that of the NBC, ABC, and CBS programs. Given that so few people watch an entire news program on the cable news channels, and that most people say they rely on these channels for political information, this means that they tune in only occasionally during a spare moment. It is unlikely that these channels are the source for much detailed learning about politics. In particular, the fact that young people are relying on cable news as opposed to network news probably means that they are just getting quick snippets as opposed to full stories that could allow them to grasp the details.

Where Have All the Water-Cooler Shows Gone?

One of the theoretical strengths of cable news is that it provides live coverage of political events whenever they occur. Young adults today have grown up in a media environment in which it has been possible to see far more live events than ever before. For example, cable news channels now show the president live almost anytime he deigns to speak in front of TV cameras. However, there is a big difference between having opportunities and taking advantage of them. The range of programming options in the narrowcasting era is so extensive that it allows one to keep one's viewing to a limited range of interests. Whereas once it was difficult to avoid major political events like a state of the union address or a presidential nominating convention, in the narrowcasting age it is a simple matter of reaching for a remote control or turning to a DVD or DVR. Growing up in a fragmented media environment with scores of TV channels and thousands of movies via Netflix has offered today's youth a rich and varied socialization experience, but also one that has enabled them to easily avoid political events.

One result of the narrowcasting revolution has been the near extinction of what the television industry calls "water-cooler shows." Such shows were so widely watched that workers who met at the office water cooler the next day could easily strike up a conversation by talking about a program that most people had seen. When there were only a few shows on TV at any given time, one show would often pull in a huge audience; today, with all the competition each show faces, the chances that one show will get a big share of viewers have been greatly reduced. An examination of Nielsen Media Research's list of the one hundred most popular shows from 1960 to 2000 illustrates this point nicely. Excluding live sporting events (which make up one-third of the list), only three shows since 1984 made the list—the finales of *Cheers*, *Seinfeld*, and *The Cosby Show*. In contrast, 16 different episodes of *The Beverly Hillbillies* from the early 1960s were on the list. To this day, the episode where Granny mistakes a kangaroo for a giant jackrabbit remains the highest-rated half-hour program since the current Nielsen system began in 1960.

Political events used to fit the bill of water-cooler shows quite frequently. If Nielsen had included events that were broadcast on multiple networks in their list, then political events would have figured prominently. For example, the typical rating that Presidents Nixon, Ford, and Carter received when they appeared on TV to give speeches or hold a press conference was 48—a higher rating than even the most popular *Beverly Hillbillies* episode. Of course, the huge audience share that political events often garnered was not due to their riveting appeal but rather to the simple fact that there used to be little in the way of viewing alternatives when regular programming on CBS, NBC, and ABC was preempted. Today, there are a multitude of alternatives to the major networks, what with the average viewer having a remote control and 189 channels from which to choose. Perhaps even more important has been the proliferation of various devices enabling viewers to choose whatever they want to watch. According to the U.S. Census, only 1 percent of homes owned a VCR in 1980, but by 1990 this device had nearly saturated the market and could be found in 69 percent of homes. VCRs, DVDs and subsequent devices freed viewers from the standard question of "What's on tonight?," allowing them to watch shows whenever they had the time. In sum, when regular programming is preempted on the major networks for a political event, most people now can turn to many alternatives if they are not interested in politics.

Young people appear to be especially likely to make use of their television remote controls. In the 2002 Pew Research Center Media Study, respondents were asked how many of the available channels they actually made use of. The mean for respondents under 30 years of age was 20 channels, compared to 15 for those between 30 and 64, and just 10 for senior citizens.[27] By switching to other programs when major political events are on, young adults have turned what used to be water-cooler shows into shows for older people. This transformation can be illustrated by an examination over time of viewing patterns of two institutionalized rituals in American presidential campaigns—political conventions and presidential debates.

Political party conventions used to receive more coverage on the major networks than the Summer Olympics. They dominated eight nights of prime-time programming every four years from 1952 to 1980. During this period, the standard practice for CBS, NBC, and ABC was to cover conventions from gavel-to-gavel—that is, whenever they were formally in session. Typically, each network provided about six hours a day of convention coverage.[28] Hence, when surveys asked whether people had seen the conventions in this period, almost everyone responded that he or she had. As can be seen in the data presented in Table 2.3, there was almost no relationship between age and having seen some convention coverage in 1972 and 1976. The extent that young people were slightly less

TABLE 2.3

Percent Watching a Portion of Party Conventions by Age, 1972–2000

	18–29	30–44	45–64	65+	65+/<30 RATIO
DEMOCRATIC CONVENTION					
1972	87	90	90	93	1.1 : 1
1976	70	80	90	92	1.3 : 1
2000	37	46	55	63	1.7 : 1
REPUBLICAN CONVENTION					
1972	70	82	79	79	1.1 : 1
1976	65	75	86	84	1.3 : 1
2000	35	44	53	62	1.8 : 1

Sources: 1972 Syracuse, NY, Survey; 1976 Erie, PA, and Los Angeles Surveys; 2000 National Annenberg Election Study.

likely to have tuned in to a convention was probably due to their having been outside, taking advantage of the summer weather. By 2000 a whole generation of young adults had grown up with narrowcasting and without ever having experienced a suspenseful political convention. The results of these changes are clearly shown in the changing demographics of the convention audience, as senior citizens were almost twice as likely as people aged 18 to 29 to report that they had watched some of the 2000 conventions.

It has been so long since anything newsworthy happened at an American political convention that college students reading this section today could justifiably ask whether the fact that their generation has largely tuned conventions out makes any difference. I would respond that their generation has missed out on tremendous opportunities for civic learning that previous generations benefited from. In addition to the marquee drama of watching the selection of the presidential and vice-presidential nominees, viewers were exposed to keynote speeches that identified the key principles of the parties, as well as to debates over the party platforms. Political conventions of the past thus provided a wide-open window into the workings of American party politics. This window has essentially been boarded up during the socialization of today's young adults.

In recent presidential campaigns, the only televised events with any sense of drama have been the presidential debates. Alan Schroeder summarizes the importance of these debates incisively:

> In a fundamental way, American politics sorely needs these infusions of drama. One reason millions of citizens have disengaged from the process—young voters especially—is that they perceive electoral politics as boring. Annoying, largely uncreative campaign commercials, coupled with superficial press coverage and overly choreographed campaign events, have rendered presidential races needlessly dull. As the only stops on the campaign trail that cannot be totally foreordained, televised joint appearances offer insights into something the public too rarely gets to see: the human side of the candidates.[29]

When Kennedy and Nixon met in four historic televised debates in 1960, they drew incredible ratings of between 58 and 61 on each occasion. Twenty years later, the one and only debate between Reagan and Carter generated the same level of audience interest, receiving a rating of 59. But with the end of the networks' captive hold on the TV audience, debate ratings have fallen substantially since 1980. In both 1996 and 2000, the presidential debates averaged an audience rating of just 28.[30]

As presidential debate ratings have declined, the representativeness of the viewing audience has naturally declined. When presidential debates were water-cooler events, young and senior citizens alike watched them. Such is the nature of water-cooler shows. As Table 2.4 shows, it is clearly the younger generations who are

TABLE 2.4
Percent Watching General Election Debates by Age, 1960–2000

	<30	30–44	45–64	65+	65+/<30 RATIO
1960 KENNEDY-NIXON DEBATES	79	80	82	69	.9 : 1
1976 CARTER-FORD DEBATES	80	83	85	83	1.0 : 1
1980 REAGAN-CARTER DEBATE	62	69	73	76	1.2 : 1
1984 1ST REAGAN-MONDALE DEBATE	67	67	71	84	1.3 : 1
1984 2ND REAGAN-MONDALE DEBATE	59	65	76	88	1.5 : 1
1984 VP DEBATE	50	57	67	69	1.4 : 1
1996 1ST CLINTON-DOLE DEBATE	38	44	61	64	1.7 : 1
1996 2ND CLINTON-DOLE DEBATE	38	44	48	61	1.6 : 1
2000 1ST BUSH-GORE DEBATE	39	48	57	67	1.7 : 1
2000 2ND BUSH-GORE DEBATE	40	47	56	64	1.6 : 1
2000 3RD BUSH-GORE DEBATE	44	47	56	67	1.5 : 1
2000 VP DEBATE	22	30	41	53	2.4 : 1

Sources: 1960, 1976, and 1996 ANES; 1984 American National Election Study
Continuous Monitoring Survey; 2000 National Annenberg Election Study.

responsible for the decline in the audience reach of presidential debates. In 2000, for example, two out of every three senior citizens interviewed said they had watched a particular presidential debate compared to only two out of five young adults. If Alan Schroeder is right in arguing that young Americans need to be convinced that politics is interesting, then it is unfortunate that they have become the least likely group to tune in to presidential debates in recent years.

On the other hand, it may well be that younger people are just more likely to consider presidential debates boring and hence deliberately don't tune in. A similar interpretation could be given for why young people are not watching TV news broadcasts. While this hypothesis is hard to disprove, I believe it is unlikely to be the case. Earlier generations were exposed to politics through news broadcasts and blockbuster political events that were hard to avoid in the era when three networks controlled 90 percent of the television audience. Many of these young adults learned through such television programming that politics was both important and interesting. Today's youth can hardly conclude that presidential debates and TV news broadcasts are boring if they have scarcely been exposed to them. And exposure seems to be the key problem in the narrowcasting age. Marshall McLuhan's famous saying about the media was that "the medium is the message."[31] In this case, the argument is essentially that the medium accounts for a lack of a message getting through to younger people. If the explanation for the trends displayed in this chapter stems from changes in the television medium, then similar patterns should be found in most other established democracies. Hence, comparative data provide a crucial test for this theory.

CAN SIMILAR PATTERNS BE FOUND IN OTHER ESTABLISHED DEMOCRACIES?

The early years of television news in other advanced industrialized countries were markedly different from those in the United States. Government-owned channels like the BBC dominated the airwaves in most other democracies. Given their government sponsorship, public service rather than profit was the driving force in the production of the news. To American eyes, the news on these channels was typically presented in a bland, "just the facts" fashion. Living near the Canadian border during the late 1970s and early 1980s, I regularly got a chance to compare the *CBC News* to that of the American networks. As a graduate student interested in public policy, I found the Canadian news broadcasts to be highly informative, often dealing with complex issues in a way that seemed unimaginable on ABC, NBC, and CBS.

Indeed, what I observed from across the border formed a sharp contrast to the academic literature I was then reading about American TV news. The standard book at the time was Edward J. Epstein's *News from Nowhere*,[32] which summarized a year of his observing NBC's news department from inside the organization. Epstein found that in their pursuit of high ratings, news shows are tailored to a fairly low level of audience sophistication. To a large extent, American TV networks define news as what is entertaining to the average viewer. A dull and complicated story would have to be of enormous importance to get on the air; in contrast, relatively trivial stories can make the cut if they are interesting enough. As former *CBS News* reporter Bernard Goldberg writes, "In the United States of Entertainment there is no greater sin than to bore the audience."[33] While I don't mean to imply that Canadian TV news was boring (after all, I was regularly watching it), it was clear to me that entertainment was not their primary goal.

With a less entertaining style of presenting the news, it should not be surprising to find that news broadcasts in other democracies were not as widely watched as American network news at its peak of popularity in the late 1960s and early 1970s. A quick look at the comparative survey data bears out this expectation. The European Communities Study (the precursor to the Eurobarometer) asked samples of five European nations how often they watched news broadcasts on television in 1970. The proportion saying they watched TV news every day was 61 percent in West Germany, 59 percent in the Netherlands, 47 percent in France, 41 percent in Belgium, and 36 percent in Italy. In contrast, 72 percent of Americans interviewed in 1967 said they watched the TV news on a daily basis.

In spite of the lower audience levels for TV news in Western Europe in 1970, the age patterns for the five countries displayed in Table 2.5 are similar to those in the United States around that time in history. Even when American network TV news was incredibly popular, young adults were still the age group least likely to report watching it every day. In part, this may stem from young adults being less likely to be regularly at home during the evening. The fact that young people (defined as ages 16 to 29 in these surveys)[34] in each of the five European countries were the least likely to habitually watch the news would seem to support such an inference. On average, senior citizens in these countries were about 18 percent more likely than young people to say that they watched the news every day, a figure not notably higher than the 12 percent difference found at the same time in the United States.

TABLE 2.5
Percent Watching the News on TV Every Day in Five European Countries, 1970

	16–29	30–44	45–64	65+	DIFFERENCE BETWEEN 65+ AND 16–29	CORRELATION WITH AGE*
NETHERLANDS	45	64	68	78	+33	.18
FRANCE	31	46	55	57	+26	.17
BELGIUM	29	38	50	49	+20	.13
ITALY	30	33	41	38	+8	.00
WEST GERMANY	54	61	67	59	+5	.07

Question wording: "Do you watch news broadcasts on television: every day, several times a week, one or two times a week, less often, or never?"

* The correlations have been calculated by recoding the question responses as follows: every day = 100; several times a week = 50; one or two times a week = 25; less often = 10; never = 0.

Source: European Communities Study, 1970.

TABLE 2.6

Percent Watching the News on TV Every Day in 11 European
Countries, 2000

	16–29	30–44	45–64	65+	DIFFERENCE BETWEEN 65+ AND 16–29	CORRELATION BETWEEN TV NEWS WATCHING AND AGE
SWEDEN	45	65	81	93	+48	.38
IRELAND	45	66	75	87	+42	.34
GERMANY	45	61	76	86	+41	.29
FRANCE	41	53	68	81	+40	.29
NETHERLANDS	56	76	83	96	+40	.28
DENMARK	53	71	85	92	+39	.34
AUSTRIA	45	60	73	83	+38	.31
BELGIUM	44	64	76	81	+37	.29
GREAT BRITAIN	56	69	82	91	+35	.29
FINLAND	66	78	86	95	+29	.21
ITALY	76	80	90	87	+11	.11

Question wording: "About how often do you watch the news on television: every day, several times a week, one or two times a week, less often, or never?"

Source: Eurobarometer, November–December 2000.

European patterns of TV news viewing by age have changed dramatically since 1970. Just like in the United States, young Europeans are now much less likely than their elders to watch the news on television. Table 2.6 displays data from a 2000 Eurobarometer study that asked a very similar question to the one asked in 1970. For the five countries that were included in both studies, senior citizens in 2000 were 34 percent more likely to report watching the TV news on a daily basis than the youngest age group—nearly twice the comparable age gap found three decades earlier. And the average correlation between frequency of TV news viewing and age in these five countries was .25 in 2000 compared to .11 in 1970. Squaring these correlations in order to obtain the percentage of explained variance reveals that this represents a five-fold increase in the degree of variation in TV news viewing habits that can be explained by age.[35] Furthermore, due to the anomalous case of Italy, the average for these five countries is probably an underestimate for Europe as a whole. Expanding the analysis to all 11 established democracies included in the 2000 Eurobarometer study reveals that Italian young people were substantially more likely to watch TV news than young people elsewhere in Western Europe. Excluding Italy, the average correlation between age and TV news viewing in 2000 was .30 in the other 10 countries.[36]

Overall, a higher percentage of Europeans said they were watching TV news every day in 2000 than in 1970. It should be noted that the question asked in both studies was a relatively broad one. Respondents could have been thinking of cable news channels as well as national broadcast news. The addition of cable news to the news menu by 2000 probably accounts for why Europeans reported more frequent news viewing in the latter period. But even with cable news included in the picture, the data show a marked bias toward an older audience for television news in Europe. As the number of channels that Europeans have to choose from has increased, younger people have been the ones least likely to choose the news.

Of course, TV news involves all sorts of subjects, and it is not necessarily the case that viewers are watching political stories. A more specific test of the narrowcasting argument can be made by looking at viewing rates of specific political events. Leadership debates prior to a general election are the one common type of political event that has been held in a number of established democracies over the past 40 years. As in the United States, these debates have provided citizens with excellent opportunities to size up and compare those who aspire to their nation's highest political office. And as has been the case with U.S. presidential debates, these televised discussions have often provided the most dramatic moments of the campaign. For example, when Canadian Liberal leader John Turner charged in a 1988 debate that Prime Minister Brian Mulroney had sold out Canada by signing the free trade deal with the United States, he scored perhaps the biggest point of the campaign. Similarly, a key event in the 2004 Australian election occurred when Labor leader Mark Latham accused Prime Minister John Howard during their one televised debate of ignoring nearby national security concerns while sending military resources to Iraq.[37]

Both these memorable leadership debates were far more likely to be seen by older voters than younger ones. As Table 2.7 shows, Canadian senior citizens were 1.8 times more likely than those under the age of 30 to say they had watched the 1988 leadership debate. In contrast, 20 years earlier in Canada there was no relationship between age and debate viewing. The data from eight Canadian election studies from 1968 to 2004 clearly show that as choices on television have proliferated, young people have opted out of watching political debates.

Although the time series for Australian debates is too limited to draw conclusions about changes over time, it is clear that young Australians have not been particularly inclined to watch more recent debates. The 2004 Australian debate was viewed by 53 percent of seniors, as compared to just 25 percent of Australians between the ages of 18 and 29. This debate faced stiff competition in its time slot from *Australian Idol*, a popular show following the format of *American Idol* in the United States. Overall, the rating

TABLE 2.7
Percent Watching Party Leader Debates in Various Countries

	<30	30–44	45–64	65+	65+/<30 RATIO
SWEDEN 1964**	66	68	70	64	1.0 : 1
NORWAY 1965*	48	56	59	62	1.3 : 1
NORWAY 1969*	55	58	65	70	1.3 : 1
CANADA 1968*	57	67	65	56	1.0 : 1
CANADA 1979*	46	51	55	58	1.3 : 1
CANADA 1984**	60	63	73	80	1.3 : 1
CANADA 1988*	42	50	64	72	1.8 : 1
CANADA 1993**	39	50	59	74	1.9 : 1
CANADA 1997**	35	46	56	66	1.9 : 1
CANADA 2000**	28	47	49	67	2.4 : 1
CANADA 2004**	37	42	55	64	1.7 : 1
GERMANY 1972**	79	90	86	73	0.9 : 1
GERMANY 1976*	74	77	78	72	1.0 : 1
GERMANY 2002 #1	41	51	57	54	1.3 : 1
GERMANY 2002 #2	38	49	62	66	1.7 : 1
NETHERLANDS 1982*	43	53	61	66	1.5 : 1
NETHERLANDS 1986*	54	53	58	71	1.3 : 1
NETHERLANDS 1989*	38	44	56	67	1.8 : 1
NETHERLANDS 1994*	42	59	53	65	1.5 : 1
NETHERLANDS 1998**	42	43	49	63	1.5 : 1
FRANCE 1988*	60	70	79	85	1.4 : 1
NEW ZEALAND 2002**	55	63	73	81	1.5 : 1
AUSTRALIA 1990*	37	53	62	73	2.0 : 1
AUSTRALIA 1993**	54	66	75	81	1.5 : 1
AUSTRALIA 1996**	45	50	63	73	1.6 : 1

(*Continued*)

TABLE 2.7 (Continued)

	<30	30–44	45–64	65+	65+/<30 RATIO
AUSTRALIA 1998*	25	33	47	67	2.7 : 1
AUSTRALIA 2001*	24	32	43	60	2.5 : 1
AUSTRALIA 2004*	25	28	32	53	2.1 : 1

*Survey asked about only one debate.

**Survey asked about multiple debates.

Source: National election studies for countries and years shown.

for *Australian Idol* was 40 percent higher than that for the so-called great debate. This came as no surprise to Australia's treasurer, Peter Costello, who told the Australian Associated Press that he had predicted that entertainment would trump politics in the ratings. Costello added that "I checked with my kids at home whether they were watching the debate or *Australian Idol* and *Idol* was winning hands down. I think a lot of people would have turned it on and had a look to see how it was going and then they'd start wavering with the finger on the remote control."[38] Although the children of the nation's treasurer were not yet old enough to vote, they were nevertheless typical of young Australian adults.

These Canadian and Australian examples are indicative of a major change in viewing patterns for leadership debates. In order to summarize the age viewing patterns, the ratio of old to young debate viewers is calculated in Table 2.7 for 28 separate election studies from eight different countries. In the 1960s and 1970s, this ratio averaged 1.1 to 1, meaning that senior citizens were only slightly more likely than young adults to tune in to a debate. By the 1980s, this ratio had changed to 1.5 to 1, and in the 1990s and early 21st century, it was 1.9 to 1. In sum, these debates are no longer shared national experiences. As in the United States, such programming appeals primarily to older people. Consequently, the concerns of young adults are not likely to be major foci of these important public policy forums.

CONCLUSION: CAN SOFT NEWS SAVE THE DAY?

For simple economic reasons, commercial television news producers would not be operating rationally if they were to ignore young adults completely. As economist James T. Hamilton points out in his book *All the News That's Fit to Sell*, two fundamental considerations for news producers are "Who cares about a particular piece of information?" and "What are others willing to pay to reach them?"[39] The results of this chapter would certainly not lead news producers to focus on young adults as the answer to Hamilton's first question. But the answer to the second question should give them some incentive to try to shape news programs in a way to attract more young people. For as Hamilton also points out, advertisers will often pay top dollar to reach young adult viewers because their purchasing decisions are less likely to be determined by brand-name loyalties.[40] Thus, if young adults aren't tuning in to traditional news broadcasts, the marketplace provides special incentives for news producers to package the news in alternative ways that might appeal to young people.

One way that the news business has adapted to the shrinking market for conventional news broadcasts has been to produce news shows designed primarily for the purpose of entertainment rather than for providing information. This TV genre has come to be known as "soft news." Some examples of soft news shows on American television include *Dateline, Inside Edition*, and *Extra*. Although these shows are not intended to serve the public interest by enlightening viewers about the details of current events,

Matthew Baum argues that under the right circumstances, they can have just that effect. He maintains that such shows have the potential to expose a broader segment of the public to "information about select high-profile political issues, including foreign policy crises, that involve scandal, violence, heroism, or other forms of sensational human drama."[41] With all sorts of entertainment shows covering a major political crisis in a different fashion than straight news shows, Baum concludes that it is more difficult than ever before to avoid exposure to the most dramatic and incredible news stories of the day. His impressive data analysis shows that the sorts of people who typically tune out politics have clearly learned a good deal about recent foreign policy crises from viewing soft news programs. The result has been a broader public knowledge of major foreign policy crises in the narrowcasting environment than in the old broadcasting era.

Baum's findings about soft news can conceivably be applied to the questions raised by this chapter. Young adults may not be paying attention to hard news shows or traditional political events, but they do like to be entertained. Thus, if soft news shows can provide entertaining coverage of political events, then they may well have the potential to save the day by making young people aware of at least some aspects of current events.

One has to be skeptical, however, of whether very many political stories will ever receive this sort of entertainment news coverage. Aside from the wars, foreign crises, and scandals that Baum examines, there is much reason to doubt whether political events ever penetrate into young people's consciousness through this sort of viewing osmosis. In short, there is good reason to suspect that the cases Baum examines are the exception rather than the rule. The next chapter attempts to establish what the norm is for political stories and how it has changed over the last few decades.

CHAPTER 3

Don't Ask Anyone Under 30

In 2012, people under the age of 30 scored the lowest in terms of factual political knowledge on 12 questions asked in the American National Election Study. On average, respondents under 30 years old answered just 37 percent of the questions correctly, as compared to 49 percent among people between the ages of 30 and 64, and 57 percent among senior citizens.

When successive generations largely fail to get into the twin habits of reading a newspaper and watching TV news, there are bound to be political consequences. Important political events often fall on deaf ears among many young people today. Such was not the case when many young people were active newspaper readers and frequently watched political coverage on TV. Now that they largely do neither of these activities, it is to be expected that older people will follow political news stories much more closely than younger people will.

When I was growing up, a common political saying was "Don't trust anyone over 30," reflecting the fact that many young people were challenging the political establishment. Today when it comes to political news stories, one could reasonably say,

"Don't ask anyone under 30," as chances are good that he or she won't have heard of these stories. Young adults today can hardly challenge the establishment if they don't have a basic grasp of what is going on in the political world.

In the first part of this chapter, we examine data on whether people of different age groups say they have followed major political events. This is important in and of itself, because if younger people aren't following what's going on in politics, they are at a sharp disadvantage in being able to direct how politicians deal with the issues of the day. Furthermore, if young people are tuned out from current events, then one of the results should be that they won't know as much about politics as their elders—a topic that is examined in the second part of this chapter.

HAVE YOUNG PEOPLE BECOME LESS LIKELY TO FOLLOW POLITICAL EVENTS?

From time to time, the American National Election Studies have asked respondents for their opinions about current events. Recognizing that not everyone will be familiar with even the most highly publicized news stories, these studies have typically first asked a filter question to ascertain whether people were aware of them. For example, in 1968 respondents were asked, "Did you happen to hear anything about what went on between the police and the demonstrators in Chicago at the Democratic Convention?" Those who replied affirmatively were then asked whether the police had used too much force or not. The principal investigators at the time were really interested in the responses to the latter question, but for the purposes of this chapter, we are interested only in the first question, that is, whether or not people followed what happened. All told, I was able to locate such questions on

10 major news stories that were asked during election years from 1948 and 2004. If recent generations have not followed current events due to the ease with which they can tune out news in the narrowcasting age, then we should find a change in attention patterns by age from the broadcasting to the narrowcasting era. The data displayed in Table 3.1 provide supporting evidence for this theory.

TABLE 3.1
Percent Following Major Events in Election Years by Age, 1948–2004

	<30	30–44	45–64	65+	DIFFERENCE BETWEEN 65+ AND <30
HEARD SOMETHING ABOUT THE TAFT–HARTLEY ACT, 1948*	58	57	58	52	–6
HEARD ABOUT THE CIVIL RIGHTS BILL, 1964	77	80	72	66	–11
HEARD DISCUSSION OF HOW THE ELECTORAL COLLEGE SYSTEM MIGHT AFFECT THE CHOICE OF THE NEW PRESIDENT BECAUSE OF WALLACE BEING IN THE RACE, 1968	52	55	54	38	–14
HEARD ABOUT WHAT WENT ON BETWEEN THE POLICE AND THE DEMONSTRATORS IN CHICAGO AT THE DEMOCRATIC CONVENTION, 1968	90	89	89	82	–8
REMEMBERED SOMETHING ABOUT THE EAGLETON CONTROVERSY, 1972	74	78	74	60	–14
HEARD ENOUGH ABOUT WHAT IS GOING ON IN SOUTH AFRICA TO HAVE AN OPINION ABOUT WHAT U.S. POLICY SHOULD BE, 1988	30	46	43	40	+10

(Continued)

TABLE 3.1 (Continued)

	<30	30–44	45–64	65+	DIFFERENCE BETWEEN 65+ AND <30
HEARD A LOT ABOUT THE CHANGES TAKING PLACE IN THE SOVIET UNION AND EASTERN EUROPE, 1990	27	37	46	53	+26
HEARD A LOT OR SOME ABOUT THE CHANGES TAKING PLACE IN THE SOVIET UNION AND EASTERN EUROPE, 1990	77	83	83	85	+8
HEARD ABOUT THE PROBLEMS IN THE SAVINGS AND LOAN BUSINESS, 1990	55	75	79	72	+17
HEARD ABOUT U.S. REPRESENTATIVES WRITING CHECKS WHEN THEY DIDN'T HAVE ENOUGH MONEY TO COVER THEM IN THEIR HOUSE BANK ACCOUNT, 1992	82	89	92	86	+4
HEARD A LOT ABOUT THE U.S. PLANNING TO HAND OVER CIVILIAN AUTHORITY TO IRAQI LEADERS, 2004	23	41	52	50	+27
HEARD A LOT OR A LITTLE ABOUT THE U.S. PLANNING TO HAND OVER CIVILIAN AUTHORITY TO IRAQI LEADERS, 2004	67	83	89	90	+23

*In 1948 the age categories were as follows: 21–34, 35–44, 45–64, 65+.

Sources: 1948–1992, American National Election Studies; June 2004, Pew Center Study.

During the broadcast era, younger people were actually *more likely* to say they had heard of major news stories of the election season than senior citizens were. The Taft–Hartley Act constraining the practices of labor unions was one of the most hotly debated matters of the 1948 campaign, with Democrats regularly referring to it as the "slave labor act." When asked about this bill during the 1948 National Election Study, senior citizens were least likely to report having heard something about it. Similarly, 16 years later when the 1964 Civil Rights Act was one of the top news stories of the day, the elderly expressed the lowest degree of awareness of it. As part of the backlash against the civil rights movement, George Wallace of Alabama mounted a significant independent candidacy for president in 1968. Because of Wallace's regional base in the Deep South, the media focused on the very real possibility that there might not be a majority winner in the electoral college vote. In the 1968 National Election Study, respondents under 30 were about a third more likely than senior citizens to say they had heard discussion about this prospect. Similarly, younger people in the same study were the most likely to say they had heard about the violence at the Democratic Convention in Chicago—hardly a surprising finding given that the violence was directed at young demonstrators. Four years later, one of the big news stories of the campaign involved the removal of Senator Eagleton from the Democratic ticket after stories emerged concerning his past treatment for clinical depression. When respondents were asked whether they remembered anything about the Eagleton controversy, once again we find a pattern of young people being more aware of a big election news story than the elderly.

Unfortunately, there were no specific questions about current events in the election surveys conducted between 1972 and 1988. During this period, the media environment changed markedly, as did the age pattern in following current events. In 1988, young people were substantially less likely than other age groups to have heard about the controversy regarding the South African racial apartheid policy. This finding is particularly noteworthy in light of the fact that opposition to apartheid in South Africa was a much-talked-about cause on college campuses throughout the 1980s. Two years later, earthshaking events were taking place throughout Eastern Europe, as the domino theory ended up applying to European communism. Though it was young people who were at the forefront of demonstrations in places such as East Berlin, Prague, and Bucharest, young Americans were the least likely to have heard about the revolutions in Eastern Europe. In this case, respondents were asked whether they had heard a lot or just some about these changes. Senior citizens were roughly twice as likely as people under 30 years of age to say that they had heard a lot about them. Furthermore, it was not just foreign events that young respondents in 1990 were unaware of. On the domestic side, young people were also the least likely to have heard about the exorbitant cost of government bailouts for the troubled savings and loan industry, which was then at the forefront of the news. Two years later, the under-30 group was slightly less likely than older people to have heard about the scandal regarding bad check writing among members of the House of Representatives. And most recently, in June 2004 a Pew Research Center survey found that young people were not following to nearly the same degree as older people the plan to hand over civilian authority to Iraqi leaders.

In sum, whereas older people used to be the least likely to follow major news stories of election years, the pattern has now been sharply reversed. Today, the older someone is, the more likely he or she is to be aware of a top news story. Of course, this pattern might be different for less prominent news stories that occur out of the spotlight of a national election. Matthew Baum's work on soft news and foreign policy might lead us to expect that young people would be relatively more aware of such issues today than they were several decades ago. A comparison of data from a 1974 survey conducted by the Chicago Council on Foreign Relations and some recent Pew Research Center polls highlights one telling test of this hypothesis.

As can be seen from Table 3.2, there was only a slight relationship between age and one's following foreign news stories in December 1974. This survey on American foreign

---

TABLE 3.2

Degree to Which People of Different Ages Followed Foreign News Stories in 1974 [entries = % responding very closely − % responding not very closely]

	18–29	30–49	50–64	65+	CORRELATION WITH AGE
WORLD FOOD CONFERENCE	+3	−4	−4	−13	−.05
WHAT'S HAPPENING IN VIETNAM THESE DAYS	−30	−41	−41	−36	−.04
CYPRUS WAR	−30	−38	−29	−39	−.02
PROBLEMS IN THE MIDDLE EAST	−2	+4	+5	−9	.00
KISSINGER'S TRIP TO CHINA	−4	−6	−2	0	.02
ARAFAT'S VISIT TO THE UN	−31	−30	−19	−28	.04
CONGRESSIONAL DEBATES ON FOREIGN DEFENSE SPENDING	−32	−30	−25	−28	.04
CONGRESSIONAL DEBATES ON FOREIGN AID	−42	−36	−26	−35	.06
ELECTIONS IN GREAT BRITAIN	−71	−72	−55	−62	.08
DISCUSSIONS ABOUT THE U.S. RECOGNIZING CUBA	−32	−30	−12	−23	.09
FORD–BREZHNEV SUMMIT MEETING	−43	−37	−15	−20	.14
AVERAGE	−29	−29	−20	−26	.03

Question wording: "How closely would you say you personally have followed news about the following events—very closely, somewhat closely, or not very closely?"

Source: Chicago Council on Foreign Relations Survey conducted by Harris, December 6–14, 1974.

policy and public opinion asked people how closely they had followed 11 of the most prominent foreign news stories of the year. Overall, the survey found that relatively few Americans paid very close attention to international relations matters. For the typical event asked about in late 1974, just 19 percent said they followed the news about it "very closely," compared to 47 percent who said "not very closely." In the shorthand index employed in Table 3.2, this registers as an index value of –28, as the percentage who did not follow the event is subtracted from the percentage that followed it very closely. Reading across the various rows, one can see that the relationship between age and following foreign news events was generally quite minimal in 1974. In three cases (the World Food Conference, Vietnam, and the Cyprus War), young people were actually the most likely to follow the news. In seven cases, older people were somewhat more likely to follow foreign policy stories, and in the case of problems in the Middle East, the correlation with age was nonexistent at .00. Overall, the average correlation between age and the 11 items that were asked about was a mere .03.

Thirty years later, the pattern had changed markedly, with attention to foreign news increasing substantially with a respondent's age. The Pew Research Center now regularly asks their survey respondents how closely they have followed the biggest news stories of the past month. These stories primarily involve domestic concerns, but in December 2002 and January 2003, they focused mostly on foreign affairs, asking about nine separate foreign stories. Overall, the American public followed these stories more closely than they had followed the major foreign stories of 1974.

Thirty-one percent said that they followed the news about the typical recent foreign policy story "very closely" compared to 19 percent in 1974, and the average percentage of people not following such stories declined from 47 to 36 percent. This results in an attention index value of –5 for 2002–2003, as compared to –28 in 1974. Such an increase in attention to foreign events is consistent with Baum's findings. But the data by age group shown in Table 3.3 present a new twist. Among adults under the age of 30, the typical level of attention paid to foreign events was nearly identical in the two eras. By contrast, the average increase in attention was 22 points for the 30 to 49 age group, 31 points for the 50- to 64-year-olds, and 34 points for senior citizens. The end result is that the average correlation between age and following foreign news was .17 for the 2002–2003 period as compared to just .03 in 1974. Granted, these were different stories, and in the more recent era America considered itself at war, whereas in the earlier period it had not. Nevertheless, there is one item that is quite similar in both periods—the Middle East—for which the correlation with age increased from .00 to .18.

One might think that young people need some substantial life experiences in order to become aware of how much things that happen far away from home in places like the Middle East may affect one's own life. But in the recent era of globalization, this seems less likely to be the case than ever before, especially considering how the Internet has made it easier than ever to obtain news about foreign events. Furthermore, one would think that the prospect of an imminent war with Iraq would make young people in the

TABLE 3.3

Degree to Which People of Different Ages Followed Foreign
News Stories in 2002–2003 [entries = % responding very
closely − % responding not too closely/not at all closely]

	18–29	30–49	50–64	65+	CORRELATION WITH AGE
DEBATE OVER THE POSSIBILITY THAT THE U.S. WILL TAKE MILITARY ACTION IN IRAQ	+15	+39	+46	+38	.12
THE WORK OF UN WEAPONS INSPECTORS IN IRAQ (DEC. 2002)	−12	+14	+25	+15	.12
THE WORK OF UN WEAPONS INSPECTORS IN IRAQ (JAN. 2003)	−11	+6	+25	+25	.14
TERRORIST ATTACKS IN KENYA AGAINST ISRAELI CITIZENS	−49	−21	−4	−14	.17
DEBATE OVER THE POSSIBILITY THAT THE U.S. WILL TAKE MILITARY ACTION IN IRAQ	+26	+33	+57	+62	.17
CONTINUED VIOLENCE IN THE MIDDLE EAST BETWEEN THE PALESTINIANS AND THE ISRAELIS	−32	−6	+14	+6	.18
THE LARGE OIL SPILL POLLUTING THE COAST OF SPAIN	−67	−42	−26	−23	.20
NORTH KOREA'S NUCLEAR WEAPONS PROGRAM	−29	−5	+25	+20	.21
POLITICAL INSTABILITY IN VENEZUELA	−87	−79	−66	−54	.25
AVERAGE	−27	−7	+11	+8	.17

Question wording: "Now I will read a list of some things that have been in the news this past month. As I read each item, tell me if you happened to follow this news story very closely, fairly closely, not too closely, or not at all closely."

Source: Pew Research Center surveys, December 2002 and January 2003.

later period more likely—not less—to follow international
relations, given that their generation would be the one called
upon to do most of the fighting.

WHAT NEWS STORIES DID YOUNG PEOPLE
FOLLOW IN 2004?

If young people are paying less attention to wars that may well involve their age group, one must wonder what news stories, if any, they are particularly attentive to. In May 2004 the Pew Research Center asked a random sample of over 5,000 Americans how much they followed 14 separate types of news stories. Out of all these news categories, there were only four that young people followed more closely than older people: 1) entertainment, 2) sports, 3) science and technology, and 4) culture and the arts. Of these four, only in the case of entertainment was the tendency for young people to follow the news more closely as strong as the tendency for older people to follow political news more closely. As David Mindich writes, the biggest change in the media environment in recent decades has been "the entertainment revolution, allowing young people basically unlimited entertainment options 24 hours a day."[42] Based on Mindich's in-depth conversations with numerous young people, he asserts that "If we want to understand why many young people don't follow the news, we need to understand the lure of entertainment."[43]

Young Americans' preference for entertainment over politics is clearly illustrated by an analysis of the Pew Research Center's data on what major news stories people paid attention to throughout 2004. During the course of the entire year, these studies asked about all sorts of news stories that were given prominent coverage in the media. Table 3.4 summarizes generational differences in attention paid to the 36 stories the Pew Research Center asked about from January through September 2004. The three news stories that young adults paid more attention to than senior citizens did were all entertainment stories—the

---

TABLE 3.4

Extent to Which Adults Under 30 Followed 2004 News Stories
Compared to Senior Citizens

Stories Young Adults Paid More Attention to than Seniors

Summer Olympics in Athens—Aug. and Sept.
Release of movie *Fahrenheit 9/11*—July
Release of movie *The Passion of the Christ*—March

Stories Young Adults Paid Slightly Less Attention to than Seniors

9/11 Commission Hearings—April
Janet Jackson Super Bowl show—Feb.
High price of gasoline—asked in five monthly surveys
Abuse of Iraqi prisoners—June
NASA landing spacecraft on Mars—Jan.

Stories Young Adults Paid Substantially Less Attention to than Seniors

Bill Clinton's book—July
Democratic Convention—Aug.
Republican Convention—Sept.
Current situation in Iraq—asked in seven monthly surveys
Gay marriage debate—Feb. and March
Terrorist bombings in Spain—March
Ethnic violence in Sudan—July
2004 presidential election—asked in seven monthly surveys
Unrest in Haiti—March
Death of Ronald Reagan—June
Reports of mad cow disease—Jan.
Saddam Hussein's court appearance—July
Code Orange alert—Jan. and Aug.
Hurricanes in the Southeast—Sept.
Transfer of power in Iraq—July

Stories Young Adults Paid Far Less Attention to than Seniors

Ads by the Swift Boat Veterans—Sept.
Reports that Libya will end its weapons program—Jan.
No WMD found in Iraq—Feb.
Conviction of Martha Stewart—March
Democratic vice-presidential nomination—July
Bill Clinton's heart surgery—Sept.
Killing of Russian schoolchildren—Sept.
President Bush's National Guard service—Feb. and Sept.
Richard Clarke's criticism of Bush administration—April
Ricin found in Senate office building—Feb.

(Continued)

TABLE 3.4 (Continued)
Recent attacks on civilians and troops in Iraq—April
Reports about the U.S. economy—Jan. and Sept.
Earthquake in Iran—Jan.

Note: For each question, an attention index was calculated for those under 30 years of age and those over 65. The index value for young adults was then subtracted from the index value for senior citizens. The categories above were determined as follows: slightly less attention = difference of 20 points or fewer; substantially less attention = difference of between 21 and 40 points; far less attention = difference of over 40 points. Items within each category are ordered from those with the lowest index difference to those with the highest.

Source: 2004 Pew Research Center surveys.

Summer Olympics and the release of two controversial movies. Similarly, the five stories that young people were almost as likely to follow as older people were of the sort that one might see covered on soft news shows such as *Extra* or *Dateline*. Janet Jackson's "wardrobe malfunction" at the Super Bowl halftime show was probably the most talked-about entertainment story of the year; the landing on Mars provided spectacular photos that were perfect for soft news shows; and the high price of gasoline was a story that anyone with a car would be interested in. Although the 9/11 Commission hearings and the abuse of Iraqi prisoners at Abu Ghraib were political stories, each had sensationalistic aspects to them that could be spun so as to provide entertainment.

In contrast, the stories that were followed far more closely by the elderly were frequently of the "Inside the Beltway" political variety. In other words, they were the sorts of stories that would receive time on shows that provide in-depth discussion of political events, such as *Washington Week in Review* on PBS or *Capital Gang* on CNN. For example, stories like Richard Clarke's criticism of the Bush administration's handling of terrorist threats and the ads by the Swift Boat Veterans criticizing Senator John Kerry's service in Vietnam provided lively discussion for such shows. The fact that older people were more attentive to such specific campaign stories certainly demonstrates that they were following the day-to-day events of the 2004 campaign more closely than were younger people.

However, if much of what young people are missing out on are stories that could come under the "Inside the Beltway" rubric, then perhaps there are relatively few consequences of the changing age demographics for political news. Though it might be crucial to have heard about the Swift Boat ads in order to understand how the 2004 campaign turned out, it wasn't necessary to know about them in order to be an informed voter. In other words, are young people really learning less of what they really need to know?

I would argue that the lack of attention young adults currently pay to mainstream media has led them to miss out on many highly consequential political stories. It should be noted that two of the 2004 stories that young adults paid relatively little attention to compared to the elderly were: 1) reports that weapons of mass destruction had not been found in Iraq and 2) reports about the condition of the U.S. economy. Surely exposure to both these stories would have helped citizens make a well-informed judgment concerning how well President Bush had performed in his first term.

The next section addresses the question of whether today's young adults are in fact less informed about politics due to their not reading newspapers, not watching TV news, and not following political stories to the same degree as previous generations of young people.

IS THIS THE LEAST POLITICALLY
KNOWLEDGEABLE GENERATION OF
AMERICAN YOUTH EVER?

Since the advent of academic survey research in the 1940s, probably the most dramatic sociological development has been the tremendous increase in public levels of formal education. This steady rise in education levels has been driven by the replacement of cohorts who averaged less than ten years of education by new generations who have averaged over 13 years of schooling.[44] If one had asked scholars in the 1940s what consequences could be expected from rising education levels, one common answer would surely have been that political knowledge would increase. In the 1948 National Election Study, the correlation between education and the measure that was developed for political knowledge was .31. Fifty-six years later, in 2004, the correlation between the same two variables was quite similar at .37. Given this relatively constant relationship between political knowledge and education, it is quite logical to expect that a better-educated population should be a more politically knowledgeable one. However, Delli Carpini and Keeter's comprehensive work on the subject, entitled *What Americans Know About Politics and Why It Matters,* finds that this has not been the case.[45] They postulate that a general decline in political engagement has offset the positive impact of rising education levels.

The findings of this book provide a more detailed explanation as to why today's well-educated young Americans have not ushered in a new age of a more politically informed public. More access to higher education has provided recent generations with the ability to learn more about politics than their grandparents were able to. But just because the potential is there doesn't mean that someone will use it. Without reading a daily newspaper, watching the TV news, or otherwise following current events, even the best-educated people will probably not pick up much knowledge about the political world. A lack of basic educational skills might make it difficult for someone to absorb political information, but even the most advanced educational skills will not help if one is not exposed to current affairs through the news.

Given their relative lack of exposure to political news and current events, young people should be falling more and more behind their elders in terms of political knowledge despite their relatively high levels of educational achievement. Table 3.5 provides American National Election Studies data from over half a century to support this hypothesis. In 18 different election studies, a variety of factual questions about politics were posed to respondents, such as, "Do you happen to know: what position this person holds? Which party now has the most members in the Senate? Who nominates federal judges?," etc. With the exception of the 1948 questions, it is a simple matter to code the responses into variables measuring whether the correct factual answer was provided or not and to calculate the percentage of correct answers within each age group. In 1948, respondents were asked a set of five questions about what was going on in the Cold War, and interviewers were responsible for classifying each person's level of information into four categories—none, low, medium, or high. These four categories were recoded from 0 to 100, and then means were calculated for each age group. Thus, in each case the entries in Table 3.5 range from 0, representing the least political knowledge, to 100, representing the most. Because the questions were different in every year, one cannot infer anything about whether overall political knowledge went up or down each year. All that these data can tell us is whether the relationship between age and political knowledge has changed, which indeed it has.

TABLE 3.5

Changing Political Knowledge/Age Relationship in United States
[entries = average % correct on factual questions]

	<30	30–44	45–64	65+	CORRELATION BETWEEN AGE AND KNOWLEDGE, CONTROLLING FOR EDUCATION
1948*	44	48	46	33	.03
1960	55	63	61	53	.06
1964	66	72	68	61	.06
1966	49	48	49	40	.09
1968	61	60	61	52	.03
1972	51	54	52	47	.11
1976	53	64	64	57	.20
1980	38	46	45	42	.15
1984	38	45	50	43	.21
1986	28	39	40	35	.21
1988	32	48	51	48	.30
1990	26	35	37	36	.27
1992	28	36	40	38	.26
1994	39	55	57	57	.26
1996	57	65	67	65	.16
1998	47	52	60	58	.22
2000	34	44	52	50	.28
2004	36	47	52	55	.27

*In 1948 the age categories were as follows: 21–34, 35–44, 45–64, 65+.

Note: See the Appendix to Chapter 3 for a list of questions employed in each year.

Source: American National Election Studies.

From 1948 through 1972, the elderly were consistently the least politically knowledgeable age group. The relative lack of political information among the elderly during this period was probably due to their rather low levels of formal education. For example, three out of five senior citizens in 1960 reported having just a grade school education (i.e., eight years or fewer of schooling). Thus, in order to understand the relationship between age and political knowledge, it is necessary to control for education. A simple way to accomplish this is to calculate a correlation that holds the level of education constant (in technical parlance, a "partial correlation"). These correlations are displayed in the far-right-hand column of Table 3.5. As expected, once the low levels of formal education among the elderly during this period are taken into account, a slight tendency is found for political knowledge to increase with age.

Since 1976, young adults have consistently scored the lowest in terms of answering these factual questions. At first, young adults were only slightly below other age groups, but this gap has widened considerably in recent years. In 2004, for example, senior citizens knew the correct answer 55 percent of the time, whereas young adults responded with the right answer just 36 percent of the time. With so many data over so many years, the most effective way of summarizing the trend is to average out the correlations, controlling for education by decade. These averages nicely illustrate how the political knowledge gap between young and old has increased over time:

1948 = .03

1960s = .06

1970s = .16

1980s = .22

1990s = .23

2000s = .28

Furthermore, a more detailed analysis of the more recent data shows that it is not just one or two items that cause young people to score lower on the index. People under 30 have consistently scored lower than other age groups on each and every factual question in recent surveys. Regardless of whether the question concerned basic civics facts, identification of current political leaders, information about presidential candidates, or knowledge of partisan control of the Congress, the result was the same: young people were clearly less well informed than the elderly. The title of this chapter—"Don't Ask Anyone Under 30"—can thus be applied not only to current political events but also to general political knowledge in the United States.

Are Young People in Other Democracies Similarly Clueless About Politics?

Young people in the United States are far from unique in not following public affairs and possessing relatively less knowledge of politics compared to older people. The same patterns have been found throughout the established democratic world in recent years. Although relevant data are not as plentiful for other democracies over time, what early data are available show that this has not always been the case.

Cross-national studies of political behavior typically focus on universal questions that will be relevant across a variety of different countries, thereby making it impossible to replicate the American analysis regarding age patterns for following current events. Thus, we will have to rely on general questions that have been asked concerning how frequently citizens follow political affairs. The authors of the classic 1959–1960 Civic Culture Study

TABLE 3.6

Degree of Following Accounts of Political and Governmental Affairs
by Age, Circa 1960 [entries = % responding regularly – %
responding never]

	18–30	31–40	41–60	61+	CORRELATION WITH AGE
USA	–4	+6	+13	+13	.11
UK	–19	–12	–3	–9	.08
WEST GERMANY	–2	+19	+9	+14	.04
ITALY	–54	–43	–55	–59	–.03

Question wording: "Do you follow the accounts of political and governmental affairs—would you say you follow them regularly, from time to time, or never?"

Source: 1959–1960 Civic Culture Study.

considered following politics on a regular basis to be an integral part of what the authors termed "the self-confident citizen" who feels capable of political participation.[46] Table 3.6 displays the age patterns for how often people said they followed accounts of political and governmental affairs in the Civic Culture Study. The summary figures indicate that there was only a slight tendency for older people to follow politics more regularly in the United States, the United Kingdom, and West Germany, with this pattern being reversed in Italy.

The 1959 data from Italy shed much light on the anomalous Italian patterns that were detailed in the previous two chapters. Unlike the case in other established democracies, recent Italian survey data show relatively little in the way of generational differences in reading newspapers and watching TV news. A close examination of how Italy compares to the rest of Western Europe reveals that what is exceptional is how infrequently older Italians read newspapers and watch TV news compared to senior citizens in other established democracies. The Italian 1959 data displayed in Table 3.6 put the experience of elderly Italians four decades later into perspective. In the 1950s, Italians fell far below Americans, British, and Germans in terms of levels of following politics. An incredible 63 percent of all Italians interviewed in 1959 said they *never* followed accounts of political and governmental affairs. Such findings led Almond and Verba to call Italy "an alienated political culture" in which "Italians tend to look upon government and politics as unpredictable and threatening forces, and not as social institutions amenable to their influence."[47] According to the socialization framework of this book, growning up in such an environment is bound to have long-term consequences. In most established democracies, today's senior citizens came of age at a time when most people were attentive to political news, and hence have maintained this habit throughout their lifetimes. However, this was not the case in Italy, and the legacy of the 1950s can be seen in later data among Italian senior citizens.

In most countries, the different socialization experiences of young and old had resulted by the beginning of the 21st century in a wide generation gap in the likelihood of following politics. Table 3.7 presents some data from the 1999–2001 World Values Study that illustrate this point very nicely. As with the wording of the question from the Civic Culture Study, the World Values Survey asked a general question concerning how often people followed politics. In every one of the 14 established democracies where this question was asked, younger people reported paying significantly less attention to political news. As shown in the far-right-hand column, the correlation between age and following politics ranged from a low of .13 in Italy to a high of .40 in Japan, with an average of .26. In simple terms that demonstrate the basic point, 65 percent of senior citizens in the typical established democracy

TABLE 3.7

Percent Who Say They Follow Politics in the News Every Day in Established
Democracies by Age, Circa 2000

	18–29	30–44	45–64	65+	DIFFERENCE BETWEEN 65+ AND 18–29	CORRELATION WITH AGE*
JAPAN	17	25	44	68	+51	.40
USA	17	29	45	63	+46	.36
NETHERLANDS	28	46	59	72	+44	.28
CANADA	13	27	46	55	+42	.30
FRANCE	37	50	66	78	+41	.30
SWEDEN	52	67	82	92	+40	.32
AUSTRIA	34	53	68	73	+39	.27
FINLAND	22	33	49	54	+32	.25
DENMARK	44	57	78	74	+30	.25
BELGIUM	27	40	58	57	+30	.21
GERMANY	42	60	68	70	+28	.18
UK	8	19	33	35	+23	.20
IRELAND	37	48	57	59	+22	.22
ITALY	37	48	57	59	+22	.13

*The "follow politics" variable has been recoded as follows for purposes of calculating correlations: every day = 7; several times a week = 3; once or twice a week = 1.5; less often = .5; never = 0.

Question wording: "How often do you follow politics in the news on TV, or on the radio, or in the daily newspapers?"

Source: 1999–2001 World Values Survey.

said that they followed politics in the news every day compared to just 30 percent of young adults.

Because young people in other democracies are not following politics, they are not learning basic political facts either. An impressive collection of survey data collected between 1959 and 2002 in various countries shows how a generation gap in political knowledge has developed. We examine data from four cross-national surveys: the Civic Culture Study (1959–1960), the Participation and Political Equality Study (1967–1971), the European Communities Study (1970), and the Comparative Study of Electoral Systems (1996–2002).

Being generally concerned with citizens' political competence, the Civic Culture Study attempted to measure how much political information respondents possessed. As Almond and Verba write, "Democratic competence is closely related to having valid information about political issues and processes, and to the ability to use information in the analysis of issues and the devising of influence strategies."[48] In their 1959–1960 surveys, they employed two sets of open-ended questions in an effort to gauge how much respondents knew about the politics of their country. The first set asked respondents to name up to three party leaders from each of the major political parties in that country. The second set noted that new presidents or prime ministers were responsible for appointing people to cabinet positions and then asked respondents whether they could recall what some of these offices are. Table 3.8 displays the mean number of party leaders and cabinet offices that people within each age category successfully named. Looking across the rows, one can see that in every case, young respondents in these four countries displayed more political information than respondents over the age of 60. Controlling for education produces a positive correlation between political information and age in the United States, but not in West Germany and Italy, and for only one of the two measures in the United Kingdom.

Because the political information measures used in the Civic Culture Study were open-ended as opposed to specific factual questions, they may just reflect the ability to recall names. Fortunately, the follow-up study a decade later, called

TABLE 3.8
Political Knowledge by Age in Four Countries, Circa 1960

	18–30	31–40	41–60	61+	CORRELATION BETWEEN AGE AND KNOWLEDGE, CONTROLLING FOR EDUCATION
MEAN NUMBER OF PARTY LEADERS IDENTIFIED					
USA	3.8	4.2	4.0	3.7	.14
UK	2.9	3.2	3.1	2.4	.08
WEST GERMANY	4.6	4.7	4.5	4.4	−.01
ITALY	2.8	2.8	2.3	1.7	−.02
MEAN NUMBER OF CABINET OFFICES IDENTIFIED					
USA	2.9	3.1	2.8	2.3	.12
UK	3.3	3.4	3.1	2.0	−.08
WEST GERMANY	3.5	3.4	3.2	2.7	−.11
ITALY	2.0	2.0	1.4	1.1	−.02

Source: 1959–1960 Civic Culture Study.

Participation and Political Equality, asked a series of direct questions in Japan and the Netherlands, as well as the same open-ended questions about party leaders in Austria. In addition, the 1970 European Communities Study asked samples in five countries if they could name the members of the Common Market (EEC), as well as their country's prime minister and foreign minister.[49] Table 3.9 presents data by age from both of these studies. The entries represent the percentage of acceptable answers. As was the case with the Civic Culture data, in every

TABLE 3.9

Political Knowledge by Age in Seven Countries, Circa 1970
[entries = percentage of acceptable answers]

	<30	30–44	45–64	65+	CORRELATION BETWEEN AGE AND KNOWLEDGE, CONTROLLING FOR EDUCATION
FRANCE 1970	58	59	63	57	.15
NETHERLANDS 1971	55	59	58	54	.10
BELGIUM 1970	55	55	58	43	.03
NETHERLANDS 1970	77	76	77	75	.02
AUSTRIA 1967	56	57	54	46	-.04
ITALY 1970	63	53	47	38	-.05
JAPAN 1967*	71	68	66	51	-.10
WEST GERMANY 1970	74	72	70	62	-.12

* Age categories for Japan were 20–29, 30–44, 45–59, 60+.

Netherlands 1971: Index based on questions asking respondents to identify the prime minister and the ministers of foreign affairs, social affairs, development aid, and the treasury.

Japan 1967: Index based on asking respondents to identify the prime minister, the age one is eligible to vote in Diet elections, and the age one is eligible to run for the Diet.

Austria 1967: Index based on adding up the number of national OVP and SPO leaders that people could name, with the maximum of eight equaling 100 percent correct.

All 1970 studies: A perfect score indicates naming all six countries that were European Economic Community members at the time, as well as the prime minister and foreign minister of one's own country.

Sources: Participation and Political Equality Study, 1967–1971; European Communities Study, 1970.

instance the elderly had the lowest score, and in a few instances young adults scored the highest. The average correlation between political information and age, controlling for education, was .00—indicating that once education was held constant, there was no relationship at all between age and political knowledge as of about 1970.

TABLE 3.10

Political Knowledge by Age in Established Democracies in Recent Years
[entries = average percentage of correct answers]

	18–29	30–44	45–64	65+	CORRELATION BETWEEN AGE AND KNOWLEDGE, CONTROLLING FOR EDUCATION
NEW ZEALAND 1996	41	46	61	67	.37
SWEDEN 1998	35	40	51	56	.33
NETHERLANDS 1998	41	48	57	56	.28
AUSTRALIA 1996	36	41	50	54	.27
UK 1997	51	63	69	68	.23
NORWAY 1997	38	45	53	54	.23
CANADA 1997	50	57	63	64	.23
IRELAND 2002	62	69	74	75	.23
FRANCE 2002	42	48	53	54	.21
SWEDEN 2002	37	47	54	52	.19
NEW ZEALAND 2002	42	47	53	55	.16
BELGIUM 1999	43	48	47	40	.11
GERMANY 1998	39	40	43	45	.10
SWITZERLAND 1999	46	49	54	53	.08
GERMANY 2002	36	35	39	37	.06

Source: Comparative Study of Electoral Systems.

In more recent times, the picture has been quite different throughout the world's established democracies. Table 3.10 presents data from 12 established democracies for which political information items have more recently been asked as part of the Comparative Study of Electoral Systems. The pattern of young adults being the least politically knowledgeable can now be readily seen in most of these countries. On average, young adults got the correct answer 43 percent of the time in the various national surveys presented in Table 3.10 compared to 55 percent for senior citizens. Controlling for education, the typical correlation between age and political knowledge was .21—almost as high as found recently in the United States.

Summary numbers of patterns of political knowledge are useful, but in order to really grasp the problem they represent, some specific examples will help to illustrate the phenomenon. Among the most interesting and telling differences I found were as follows:

- Seventy-three percent of Australian senior citizens knew that no one may stand for parliament unless they pay a deposit, compared to 27 percent of young adults.
- Eighty-one percent of Swiss senior citizens could name the president of the confederation, compared to 54 percent of young adults.
- Eighty-three percent of German senior citizens could name the foreign minister, compared to 55 percent of young adults.
- Sixty-five percent of Canadian senior citizens could name the minister of finance, compared to 22 percent of young adults.
- Sixty percent of Swedish senior citizens could identify the photo of the leader of the Green Party, compared to 22 percent of young adults—even though young people were more likely to vote for this party.
- Eighty percent of Norwegian senior citizens could recall who had been president of the Storting (parliament) for the last four years, compared to 39 percent of young adults.
- Sixty percent of Irish senior citizens could identify the name of Ireland's European commissioner, compared to 35 percent of young adults.

- Sixty percent of New Zealand's senior citizens understood how the country's new mixed-member proportional (MMP) electoral system worked, compared to 34 percent of young adults.

Exceptions to the general pattern of the young being the least knowledgeable were rare, but there were some. In Canada, young people were 9 percent more likely to know who had been the country's first female prime minister; in Switzerland, the young were 10 percent more likely to know how many signatures are required for a referendum; in Germany, young people were 8 percent more likely to know the number of EU members; and in France, the young were 3 percent more likely to know that deputies were not elected via proportional representation. These political facts that young people were relatively aware of show that today's youth are not doomed to be politically clueless forever. The problem is that these days, young people get such little exposure to political events and news reports that few such facts get through to them.

CONCLUSION: THE IMPACT OF POLITICAL KNOWLEDGE

It is hardly young people's fault that their generation has learned less about politics than any other generation since the beginning of survey research. It is often said in the culinary business, "You are what you eat." In the news business, it could well be said, "You know what you follow." And in the case of young adults, what they follow closely is entertainment, not politics. Therefore, surveys have found that young Americans are the most likely to know things like the winner of *American Idol*, the name of Homer Simpson's hometown, or who won the most recent Super Bowl.[50]

Regardless of whether the phenomenon of young people not following political news stems from deliberate or circumstantial avoidance, the relative lack of political knowledge that is the result has real consequences. Thomas Jefferson once said that there has never been, nor ever will be, a people who are politically ignorant and free. If this is indeed the case, write Stephen Bennett and Eric Rademacher, then "we can legitimately wonder what the future holds if Xers remain as uninformed as they are about government and public affairs."[51] While this may well be an overreaction, there definitely are important consequences when citizens lack political information. In *What Americans Know About Politics and Why It Matters*, Michael Delli Carpini and Scott Keeter make a strong case for the importance of staying informed about public affairs. Political knowledge, they argue: 1) fosters civic virtues, such as political tolerance; 2) helps citizens to identify what policies would truly benefit them and to incorporate this information into their voting behavior; and 3) promotes active participation in politics.[52] It is certainly the case that due to youths' lack of information about politics compared to their elders, a significant generation gap has emerged in terms of turnout in many established democracies. This development will be examined in detail in the next chapter.

Appendix to Chapter 3

List of questions used for knowledge scales in Table 3.5.

1948: Respondents were asked the following set of questions: "Now, we'd like to find out a little bit of what people have heard about what is going on between ourselves and Russia. Do you happen to know whether the U.S. has been doing anything to try to stop Russia from getting control of other countries? What have we been doing? Have you heard anything about the troubles we have been having with Russia in Berlin? Do you happen to know whether we have been doing anything to help Western Germany get back on her feet? What are we doing?" Responses were coded in 1948 into the following four categories: no information, low information, medium information, and high information. In order to create a 0-to-100 scale, these categories have been recoded to 0, 33, 66, and 100.

1960: 1) where Nixon was from; 2) Nixon's age [40s]; 3) Nixon's class [middle]; 4) Nixon's religion [Protestant, Quaker]; 5) where JFK was from; 6) JFK's age [40s]; 7) JFK's class [upper]; 8) party in control of the House before the election; 9) party in control of the House after the election

1964: 1) where Goldwater was from; 2) where Johnson was from; 3) Goldwater's religion; 4) Johnson's religion; 5) party in control of the House before the election; 6) party in control of the House after the election; 7) whether Johnson had supported Civil Rights Act; 8) whether Goldwater had supported Civil Rights Act

1966: 1) able to name a Supreme Court justice; 2) party in control of the House before the election; 3) party in control of the House after the election

1968, 1976, 1980: 1) party in control of the House before the election; 2) party in control of the House after the election

1972: 1) know how many times a president can be elected; 2) know the length of a Senate term; 3) know the length of a House term; 4) party in control of the House before the election; 5) party in control of the House after the election

1984: 1) party in control of the House before the election; 2) party in control of the House after the election; 3) party in control of the Senate before the election; 4) party in control of the Senate after the election

1986: 1) identify Bush; 2) identify Weinberger; 3) identify Rehnquist; 4) identify Volcker; 5) identify Dole; 6) identify O'Neill; 7) party in control of the House before the election; 6) party in control of the Senate before the election

1988: 1) identify Ted Kennedy; 2) identify Schultz; 3) identify Rehnquist; 4) identify Gorbachev; 5) identify Thatcher; 6) identify Arafat; 7) identify Wright; 8) party in control of the House before the election; 9) party in control of the House after the election

1990: 1) identify Quayle; 2) identify George Mitchell; 3) identify Rehnquist; 4) identify Gorbachev; 5) identify Thatcher; 6) identify Mandela; 7) identify Foley; 8) party in control of the House before the election; 9) party in control of the House after the election

1992: 1) identify Quayle; 2) identify Rehnquist; 3) identify Yeltsin; 4) identify Foley; 5) know that the Supreme Court decides constitutionality; 6) know that the president nominates judges; 7) party in control of the House before the election; 8) party in control of the Senate before the election

1994: 1) identify Gore; 2) identify Rehnquist; 3) identify Yeltsin; 4) identify Foley; 5) know that the Supreme Court decides constitutionality; 6) know that the president nominates federal judges; 7) party in control of the House before the election; 8) party in control of the Senate before the election

1996: 1) identify Gore; 2) identify Rehnquist; 3) identify Yeltsin; 4) identify Gingrich; 5) party in control of House before the election; 6) party in control of House after the election

1998: 1) identify Gore; 2) identify Rehnquist; 3) identify Yeltsin; 4) identify Gingrich; 5) party in control of the House before the election; 6) party in control of the Senate before the election

2000: 1) where Bush was from; 2) where Gore was from; 3) party in control of the House before the election; 4) party in control of the Senate before the election; 5) Lieberman's religion [Jewish]; 6) identify William Rehnquist; 7) identify Tony Blair; 8) identify Janet Reno; 9) identify Trent Lott

2004: 1) identify Hastert; 2) identify Cheney; 3) identify Blair; 4) identify Rehnquist; 5) House majority before the election; 6) Senate majority before the election

CHAPTER 4

Where Have All the Young Voters Gone?

In the 2014 election, just 10 percent of Delaware residents between the ages of 18 and 29 voted as compared to 56 percent among senior citizens according to data compiled from actual turnout records made available by Delaware's Election Commissioner.

Why does anyone ever vote? Rational choice theorists have long pointed out that the chance of any one individual's vote making a difference to the outcome is extraordinarily slight. What instead drives many people to vote is simply that for one reason or another, they care who wins.[53] Such participation can be likened to spectators at a sporting event. Just like with voting, the involvement of any particular fan is hardly crucial to the outcome. While democracy wouldn't exist without some citizens going to the polls, without fans at a game there wouldn't be a home field advantage. Individually, a sports spectator gets the benefits of rooting in person for his or her team, enjoying the spectacle, and seeing firsthand who wins. Similar benefits can be posited for voters.

People who have a clear personal interest in who governs and what the government does are therefore more inclined to vote, just as people with a favorite team are more likely to attend a sporting event involving their team.

But if you don't follow the sport and don't have a favorite team, then you are less likely to go to the games. Likewise in the world of politics, people who don't follow the news and current events are less likely to participate in elections for a number of similarly fundamental reasons. If you don't follow political news, then you are less likely to 1) know who is running for various public offices, 2) be informed about what the candidates stand for, 3) have an interest in the issues that are being debated, and 4) realize what is at stake in an election—both for yourself personally and for the country. Thus with recent generations establishing modern lows for newspaper reading, TV news watching, and knowledge of public affairs (as shown in the previous three chapters), it is to be expected that their turnout rates should be falling substantially behind their elders.

Indeed, as this chapter shows, getting young adults to the polls these days is a lot like getting someone who generally doesn't follow sports to watch a football game. This problem is particularly evident in elections of lesser importance, such as midterm elections, primaries, and local elections. These elections—commonly referred to in political science as "second-order elections"—attract less media attention. Therefore, people who pay minimal attention to politics often have little reason to care about them. Elections for the presidency of the United States or a nation's parliament, on the other hand, are more like the Super Bowl. Just as some people who don't follow football will end up watching the Super Bowl because of all the hoopla surrounding it, so will some people who rarely follow public affairs get caught up enough in election fever to vote. As will be seen in the first part of this chapter, getting young adults to vote in Super Bowl-style elections (commonly referred to as "first-order elections" in political science) is becoming more and more of a problem in the United States and many other established democracies.

The second part of this chapter then turns to second-order elections, where the age gap in terms of electoral participation has reached alarming levels in many countries.

Turnout by Age in American Presidential Elections Since 1964

In 1964, the U.S. Census Bureau began a series of studies regarding registration and turnout in U.S. elections. A primary motivation of the Census Bureau in examining this topic was to measure racial differences in turnout that were widely perceived to be a blemish on the practice of American democracy. Blacks at the time were substantially underrepresented at the polls, and the 1964 Census Bureau study provided some hard data on the state of the problem. In the South, this survey found that 59 percent of Whites reported that they had voted, compared to just 44 percent among non-Whites. In the standard shorthand used throughout this chapter, such a turnout discrepancy translates into a turnout ratio of about 1.3 to 1. Or, to put it another way, Southern Whites were roughly 30 percent more likely to vote than were Southern non-Whites in 1964. Such a large gap in turnout rates no doubt helped persuade the U.S. Congress to end racial discrimination in registration practices in the South by passing the 1965 Voting Rights Act.

Interestingly, the cover page of the Census Bureau's report regarding turnout in 1964 highlighted turnout differences between the young and the old, perhaps because this was a much less expected finding.[54] A careful reading of this report reveals that the difference between the national turnout rate of 21-to-24-year-olds and those over 65 in 1964 was just as wide as the racial differences in the South. This finding validated the concerns about low youth turnout expressed by President Kennedy's Commission on Registration and Voting Participation. The Commission's November 1963 report argued that by the time young people turn 21, many "are so far removed from the stimulation of the educational process that their interest in public affairs has waned." The report went on to warn that "Some may be lost as voters for the rest of their lives" and to recommend that in order to address this problem, "states should carefully consider reducing the minimum voting age to 18."[55]

As the movement to lower the voting age to 18 grew in strength over the next eight years, the general opinion was that this would ameliorate the problem of relatively low youth turnout—not make it worse. Jane Eisner's summary of the Senate Judiciary Committee hearings on the proposal concludes that there was "a palpable belief that these new voters would improve the political system with their intelligence, idealism, and energy."[56] Historian Alexander Keyssar notes that the ratification process for the Twenty-sixth Amendment, which lowered the voting age to 18, was the fastest in American history.[57] When this amendment was certified in 1971, President Nixon remarked, "The country needs an infusion of new spirit from time to time. As I stand here, I sense that we can have confidence that America's new voters will provide what this country needs."[58]

Such high hopes for voting participation among 18-to-20-year-olds were quickly dispelled when this group was first able to vote in the Nixon–McGovern contest of 1972, as their turnout rate of 48 percent was the lowest for any age group that year. Ironically,

TABLE 4.1

Turnout by Age in Presidential Elections, 1964–2004

	18–20	21–24	25–34	35–44	45–54	55–64	65+	65+/21–24 RATIO
1964	—	51	65	73	76	76	66	1.3 : 1
1968	—	50	63	71	75	75	66	1.3 : 1
1972	48	51	60	66	71	71	64	1.3 : 1
1976	38	46	55	63	68	70	62	1.3 : 1
1980	36	43	55	64	68	71	65	1.5 : 1
1984	37	44	55	64	68	72	68	1.5 : 1
1988	33	38	48	61	67	69	69	1.8 : 1
1992	39	46	53	64	69	72	70	1.5 : 1
1996	31	33	43	55	62	68	67	2.0 : 1
2000	28	35	44	55	62	67	68	1.9 : 1
2004	41	42	47	57	64	70	69	1.7 : 1

Source: U.S. Census Bureau surveys.

what was then a disappointing result for the 18-to-20-year-old turnout now looks impressive in light of subsequent results. As can be seen from the Census Bureau's survey data displayed in Table 4.1, in the first eight elections after 1972, the turnout rate of 18-to-20-year-olds averaged just 35 percent. Given that the turnout rate for the under-21 crowd has consistently been the lowest of any age group, the lowering of the voting age has clearly contributed to the downturn in U.S. turnout in recent decades.

It might be theorized that 18-to-20-year-olds will always vote in substantially lesser numbers than people a few years older due to life-cycle factors. Highton and Wolfinger outline a series of major life changes that people under the age of 25 commonly go through while they sort out their lives, each of which might make it less likely for them to vote.[59] However, their analysis of the

1996 Census Bureau data set demonstrates that such lifestyle transitions can account for only a small portion of the age differential in turnout. Thus, it would be a mistake to conclude that low turnout among 18-to-20-year-olds was inevitable and should have been foreseen by the advocates of the Twenty-sixth Amendment. Indeed, there have been three cases—1972, 1996, and 2004 —in which the turnout rate for Americans under the age of 21 was not significantly different from the rate for those between the ages of 21 and 24.

The problem with getting America's youngest eligible voters to the polls has been that they have gotten the least exposure to political events while growing up due to the ongoing changes in media habits outlined in previous chapters. As these changes in the media environment have played out over the years, the age distribution of Americans who participate in presidential elections has become much more skewed toward the elderly. Between 1964 and 1976, the ratio between the turnout rate of people over 65 and that of those between the ages of 21 and 24 was a consistent 1.3 to 1. Since then, this ratio has gotten much worse, reaching a high of 2.0 to 1 in the particularly dull 1996 contest between Clinton and Dole. The 2004 election saw a modest improvement to a 1.7 to 1 ratio, as turnout rose most notably among the young (who, of course, had the most potential for such an increase due to their previous abysmal turnout rates). But in spite of this recent upsurge of electoral participation among young adults, the situation remains a sorry one for American democracy. If a 1.3 to 1 turnout ratio between Whites and Blacks in the South was a dreadful state of affairs in the early 1960s, then a 1.7 to 1 ratio between the old and the young is certainly a serious problem in the early 21st century.

Furthermore, the problem of lower turnout is no longer mostly confined to the under-25 age group. Even with the increase in turnout rates in 2004, the majority of people between the ages of 25 and 34 still did not vote. Whereas differences in turnout between this age group and seniors were negligible in 1964 and 1968, seniors were more than 1.6 times as likely to vote as those aged 25 to 34 in 2004. A similar transformation can be found among Americans between the ages of 35 to 44. Between 1964 and 1976, this group consistently had a higher turnout rate than people over 65. Since then, a substantial gap has opened up, as turnout among this middle-aged group has fallen dramatically. In each of the last three presidential elections, the ratio between the turnout rate of seniors and the 35-to-44-year-old group has been 1.2 to 1.

In short, there has been a dramatic change in the relationship between age and turnout since the Census Bureau surveys started keeping track of who votes in America. Because these surveys have a huge sample size of roughly 100,000 cases, it is possible to graph participation rates by age quite precisely. Figure 4.1 presents smoothed curves for the age–turnout relationship in three elections: 1972, 1996, and 2004. In 1972 (the first year for which precise age data are available given that the raw data for the 1964 and 1968 surveys have been lost), one can see that turnout went up gradually about 20 percentage points from age 18 to age 44, then leveled off, and finally started to decline after the age of 60. In 1996, the lowest-turnout election in recent times, turnout went up far more steeply with age, rising about 40 percentage points from age 18 to age 60 and then leveling off at a rate of about 70 percent through age 80. Finally, the age–turnout curve for 2004 illustrates how an increase in turnout is now bound to come mostly from the youngest adults. Yet, even the extraordinary intensity with which the 2004 presidential election was contested failed to motivate young and middle-aged Americans to go to the polls in nearly the same percentages as seen in the landslide 1972 contest. In contrast, turnout rates among senior citizens were actually higher in the two more recent

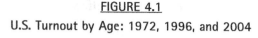

FIGURE 4.1
U.S. Turnout by Age: 1972, 1996, and 2004

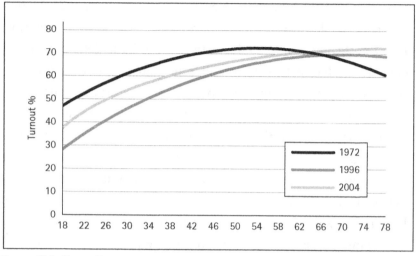

Source: U.S. Census Bureau surveys.

years shown in Figure 4.1 than in 1972. Political scientists used to write that the frailties of old age led to a decline in turnout after one became eligible for Social Security. Now an examination of the Census Bureau survey data shows that such a decline occurs only after 80 years of age. (Due to the way the Census Bureau codes these age categories together, these data are not displayed in the figure.[60]) The greater access to medical care provided to today's seniors must surely be given some of the credit for this change, helping to keep them in sufficiently good health to vote. One could certainly tell young citizens this today as an illustration of how politics really can make a difference.

The changing relationship between age and turnout that has been found in the United States leads us to question whether a life cycle actually exists for electoral participation. A true life-cycle pattern would be roughly the same throughout different time periods. This is not to imply that turnout should remain exactly the same over time, but rather that the participation of each age group should change by roughly the same amount from year to year. Clearly, this has not been the case in the United States.

Comparative data provide a key test for the existence of a life-cycle effect for turnout. If one's stage in life really influences one's likelihood of voting, then this pattern should be found to be similar over time in most established democracies. We thus now turn to an examination of participation patterns in first-order elections in other countries.

TURNOUT BY AGE IN PARLIAMENTARY ELECTIONS: CHANGE OVER THREE DECADES

The early comparative research on parliamentary elections hardly mentioned turnout at all. Scholarly neglect of this subject occurred mainly because, unlike in the United States, turnout levels were typically very high elsewhere in the established democratic world. With almost everyone voting, there was not much concern about analyzing the relatively small percentage of people who didn't vote. If American reformers who advocated lowering the voting age had found it difficult to conceive how expanding the franchise might lessen overall turnout levels, then those who advocated a similar move around the same time in other countries would have found it downright implausible. Turnout problems were something that America might have had due to its burdensome registration procedures, but other established democracies (except tiny Switzerland) had no such worries. Citizens who were eligible to vote almost always did so; it mattered little whether they were young or old.

Table 4.2 presents turnout data by age group from surveys conducted circa 1972 in 16 established democracies. This time frame was selected for two reasons: 1) it was about the time when many other countries also lowered their voting age to 18, and 2) it was the earliest time period for which survey data on

TABLE 4.2
Percent Reporting Casting a Ballot by Age in Established Democracies, Circa 1972

	<30	30–44	45–64	65+	OLDEST/YOUNGEST RATIO
USA 1972	53	65	71	64	1.2 : 1
SWITZERLAND 1971	48	66	67	55	1.1 : 1
GREAT BRITAIN FEB. 1974	82	88	92	89	1.1 : 1
FINLAND 1972	85	91	95	90	1.1 : 1
NETHERLANDS 1972	85	90	92	90	1.1 : 1
NORWAY 1969	90	94	97	94	1.0 : 1
CANADA 1974	83	83	88	86	1.0 : 1
ITALY 1972	95	97	96	97	1.0 : 1
AUSTRIA 1971	97	97	98	99	1.0 : 1
NEW ZEALAND 1975	93	97	98	95	1.0 : 1
DENMARK 1971	91	96	94	91	1.0 : 1
FRANCE 1967	89	90	92	89	1.0 : 1
SWEDEN 1973	92	95	95	92	1.0 : 1
JAPAN 1967	81	93	93	80	1.0 : 1
IRELAND 1977	82	88	83	79	1.0 : 1
WEST GERMANY 1972	98	98	97	95	1.0 : 1

Notes: The voting age in Finland, Sweden, and Japan was 20; in Norway, France, Denmark, Italy, and Switzerland it was 21; all others had voting age of 18. Data from Ireland represent the percentage saying they were "certain to vote." The Irish age categories were 18–34, 35–44, 45–64, 65+. Age categories for Denmark were 21–29, 30–49, 50–64, 65+.

Sources: Various National Election Studies; U.S. Census Bureau Study; Finland, Austria, and Italy: Political Action Study; Ireland: NOP Preelection Poll.

elections were available from almost all of the world's established democracies.[61] Looking down the column for people under 30, one can clearly see that most countries had no trouble at all in getting young people to the polls in this era. Only the United States and Switzerland had turnout rates below 80 percent among young adults. Excluding these two outliers, the average reported turnout rate for people under 30 was a very healthy 89 percent during the period around 1972. Granted, this represents an overreport of voter turnout, as surveys commonly find that more people say they voted than we know actually did. However, there is no reason to suspect that young people would have been consistently more likely to over-report turnout than older people. And the key finding in the circa 1972 data is that there was not much of a discrepancy between the turnout rates of the elderly and the young. The United States was the only country in which the ratio between the two groups was above 1.1 to 1; in 11 of the 16 countries, the two groups had roughly equal turnout levels. To those who take a defeatist attitude regarding the current problem of low youth turnout and argue that this is just a difficult time in life to get people to go to the polls, these data send a clear message: not so long ago the participation rate of young people in parliamentary elections was quite healthy.

Since then, the picture has changed markedly in many countries. The United States is certainly not alone in having a problem getting young people to the polls. Table 4.3 presents data collected around the turn of the century in 18 established democracies. In nine of these countries, people over 65 were at least 1.3 times more likely to have voted than adults under the age of 30. Or, if one simply looks at percentages, one finds that the turnout rate of young adults was at least 10 percent below that of senior citizens in 11 countries. Of the other seven established

TABLE 4.3
Percent Reporting Casting a Ballot by Age Categories in Advanced Industrialized Democracies Around the Turn of the Century

	<30	30–44	45–64	65+	OLDEST/YOUNGEST RATIO
JAPAN 2003*	36	55	71	71	2.0 : 1
USA 2000	36	52	64	68	1.9 : 1
GREAT BRITAIN 2001*	39	57	69	71	1.8 : 1
IRELAND 2002	59	82	87	87	1.5 : 1
CANADA 2000	63	82	91	92	1.5 : 1
NORWAY 2001*	59	78	82	84	1.4 : 1
NEW ZEALAND 2002*	63	76	84	88	1.4 : 1
SWITZERLAND 2003	57	57	72	81	1.4 : 1
FRANCE 2002	67	78	86	84	1.3 : 1
FINLAND 2003	68	80	87	83	1.2 : 1
GERMANY 2002*	70	79	83	82	1.2 : 1
AUSTRIA 2002	82	90	92	90	1.1 : 1
SWEDEN 1998	83	89	91	90	1.1 : 1
NETHERLANDS 1998	88	91	92	94	1.1 : 1
DENMARK 2001*	81	85	89	83	1.0 : 1
AUSTRALIA 2004**	97	98	98	99	1.0 : 1
ITALY 2001	89	92	93	86	1.0 : 1
BELGIUM 2004**	89	98	97	92	1.0 : 1

*Validated records of actual participation used here.

*Compulsory voting in effect.

Notes: Age categories were slightly different for the following countries—Germany: 18–29, 30–44, 45–60, 60+; Ireland: 18–34, 35–44, 45–64, 65+; Norway, Denmark: 18–29, 30–39, 40–59, 60+.

Sources: Comparative Study of Electoral Systems unless otherwise noted; Italy, Austria, and Finland: European Social Survey 2002/3; New Zealand Election Study; British Election Study; U.S. Census Bureau Study; Irish Central Statistics Office; Statistiches Bundesamt (Germany); Statistics Norway; Japan National Election Management Commission; Jorgen Elklit, Palle Svensson, and Lise Togeby, "Why Is Voter Turnout Not Declining in Denmark?" Paper presented at the 2005 APSA meeting.

democracies covered in Table 4.3, Belgium and Australia require all citizens to show up at the polls for national elections. Only Italy, Austria, Sweden, Denmark, and the Netherlands have recently been successful in getting young people to vote in satisfactory numbers without compelling them to do so. Why these countries have not experienced the problem of low youth turnout is an interesting puzzle that I leave to others to investigate.[62] For the purposes of this book, the major point I want to get across is that the problem of low youth turnout is by no means just an American one. To those who propose explanations for why turnout rates have declined among young Americans based on particular events in U.S. politics, I ask them to consider why similar trends can also be found in Japan, Great Britain, Ireland, Canada, Norway, New Zealand, Switzerland, France, Finland, and Germany.

THE TURNOUT GAP IN AMERICAN
SECOND-ORDER ELECTIONS

As Mark Franklin writes, "Turnout appears to vary because of variations in the character of elections."[63] Franklin insightfully points out that what differentiates low- from high-turnout elections are not the characteristics of the eligible electorate but rather the nature of the elections themselves. Because second-order elections are less likely to decide crucial issues, or get as much media coverage as presidential or parliamentary elections, they just don't appear as important to citizens. And when elections don't appear important, individuals who are less attuned to political news may not hear enough about them to feel that they have any stake in who wins. As outlined in the first three chapters, young adults these days are particularly likely to fit this description. Hence, it should be expected that age differences in turnout will be even larger in second-order elections than in first-order ones.

Five U.S. states now regularly report voting participation rates of registered voters within various age categories. Advances in computer technology have made it relatively simple to computerize voter registration lists. Given that citizens are required to state their date of birth in order to establish their eligibility to vote, age is one variable that is always included in these computerized records. Once an election is completed, local registrars add information regarding who voted, which is a crucial piece of information for them because Congress has specified that no one can be purged from a registration list if he or she has voted in the past four years.[64] With these columns of data in their computer banks, a basic cross-tabulation reveals precisely how many of those registered within each age group actually voted. Table 4.4 presents the data on turnout by age that Iowa, Georgia, Delaware, South Carolina, and Alaska have reported on their websites for elections held between 2000 and 2004. It should be noted that these percentages are based only on people who have gone to the trouble of getting on the voter registration rolls. Were one to take into account the fact that young Americans are the least likely to be registered, the turnout gap between the young and the old would be even greater than that displayed in Table 4.4. However, the major point of this table is to illustrate differences between types of elections, and these official turnout statistics clearly show that young people's participation rates fall off most sharply when elections are not hotly contested.

Age bias at the polls was far more pronounced in the 2002 midterm election than in either of the presidential elections in

TABLE 4.4

Official Turnout Figures of Registered Voters by Age in Presidential Versus Second-Order Elections in Five States, 2000–2004

	18–24	25–34	35–49	50–64	65+					OLDEST/YOUNGEST RATIO
IA 2004	58	61	78	86	84					1.4 : 1
IA 2000	44	54	75	84	83					1.9 : 1
IA 2002	22	35	58	72	73					3.3 : 1

	18–24	25–29	30–34	35–39	40–44	45–49	50–54	55–59	60–64	65+	OLDEST/YOUNGEST RATIO
GA 2004	56	63	71	75	77	79	81	83	84	80	1.4 : 1
GA 2000	44	55	64	69	72	75	78	79	81	77	1.8 : 1
GA 2002	22	33	44	51	56	60	65	68	71	68	3.1 : 1

	18–29	30–39	40–49	50–64	65+					OLDEST/YOUNGEST RATIO
DE 2004	55	57	68	77	75					1.4 : 1
DE 2000	48	58	70	80	76					1.6 : 1
DE 2002	19	31	46	59	64					3.4 : 1

(Continued)

TABLE 4.4 (Continued)

	18–21	22–44	45–64	65+	OLDEST/YOUNGEST RATIO
SC 2004	62	63	77	74	1.2 : 1
SC 2000	49	55	73	70	1.4 : 1
SC 2002	28	43	65	67	2.4 : 1
SC 2004 PRIMARY	13	15	31	39	3.0 : 1
SC 2000 PRIMARY	9	11	24	31	3.4 : 1
SC 2002 PRIMARY	10	16	30	39	3.9 : 1

	18–24	25–34	34–44	45–54	55–64	65+	OLDEST/YOUNGEST RATIO
AK 2004	53	55	66	74	76	75	1.4 : 1
AK 2000	46	48	61	69	70	70	1.5 : 1
AK 2002	26	35	51	63	67	66	2.5 : 1
AK 2004 PRIMARY	11	14	24	35	43	48	4.4 : 1
AK 2002 PRIMARY	9	12	21	31	36	40	4.4 : 1
AK 2000 PRIMARY	7	8	15	22	28	35	5.0 : 1

Sources: Secretary of State websites for Iowa, Georgia, Delaware, South Carolina, and Alaska.

all five states. The data from Iowa provide a perfect example. As can be seen in the upper-right corner of Table 4.4, the ratio between the turnout rate of senior citizens and those aged 18 to 24 in Iowa increased from 1.9 : 1 in the 2000 election to 3.3 : 1 in the 2002 midterm election. Although the turnout of seniors in Iowa had the most room for drop-off, given their high turnout in 2000, their participation remained strong in 2002—falling slightly from 83 to 73 percent. In contrast, turnout among young Iowans who were registered was cut in half, dropping from a rather poor showing of 44 percent in 2000 to an abysmal 22 percent in 2002. The dreadful turnout of young Iowans in 2002 was unfortunately quite typical of the pattern throughout the country. Looking at the other four states shown in Table 4.4 reveals that the highest turnout rate among the youngest age category was just 28 percent for 18-to-21-year-olds in South Carolina.

Yet, the poor midterm participation rate among young Americans looks relatively rosy compared to their widespread neglect of primary elections. The states of South Carolina and Alaska consistently reported turnout rates of about 10 percent for the youngest age group in 2000, 2002, and 2004. By contrast, the typical turnout rate for senior citizens in primaries in these states was about 40 percent. One reason that young Americans often do not participate in primaries is that in many states they are closed to voters who are not registered as Democrats or Republicans, and young people are the most likely to be political independents. But each of these two states allows independents to choose a ballot from one or the other party for primary elections even though they aren't registered as a member of that party. Nevertheless, young registered citizens seem to treat primary elections like a party they have not been invited to. The result is that older voters are largely in charge of picking the candidates who will appear on the November ballot.

Although most of the data in Table 4.4 regarding young Americans' voting participation rates reflect bad news, there is one bright spot in the official turnout statistics from these five states. The figures from the 2004 election demonstrate that when a close and interesting contest for president occurs, the turnout of young people will go up dramatically (at least among those who are registered). The problem is that this is the exception, not the rule. In the complex, multilayered American political system, which provides for frequent opportunities to go to the polls, most elections are second-order ones. Just tuning in to a particularly exciting Super Bowl doesn't make one a football fan; similarly, just participating in one especially hotly contested election doesn't make a group an integral part of the American political process. As the National Football League and its sponsors make plans for its next season, they are hardly likely to take into account the views of people who tuned in only to the Super Bowl. Likewise, politicians are bound to pay only marginal attention to voters who show up only for a high-intensity presidential election, concentrating far more on people who can be counted on to vote on a regular basis.

The widespread availability of voting history records enables political campaign strategists to quite easily identify these habitual voters. Traditional party organizations who used to sweep whole neighborhoods have been largely replaced by more sophisticated voter targeting. As Alan Ware has written, this switch from party to high-tech campaigning "helped to create 'two nations' in the electorate: those who received considerable attention from candidates and those who were ignored."[65] Many campaigns will bother to contact only those voters who have regularly shown up at the polls in past elections. Such a focus creates a mobilization bias in favor of older voters.

An analysis of 5,354,376 actual voter history records between 2000 and 2003 from Los Angeles, San Francisco, and Orange County, California, illustrates just how pronounced this bias is.[66] Table 4.5 displays the percentage of registered voters in each age category who voted in all three major contests from 2000 to 2003 —the 2000 presidential election, the 2002 midterm election, and the 2003 recall election that made Arnold Schwarzenegger governor. Among those who were 18 to 24 years old (as of 2000) and registered to vote in California throughout this whole period, only 14 percent voted in all three elections. By contrast, among citizens who were between 65 and 79 years of age, an impressive 60 percent voted three out of three times. The electoral participation age gap appears even wider once one takes into account the proportion of each age that was registered to vote. As California campaigns geared up for the 2004 primary, the odds of a citizen born between 1921 and 1935 being on a target list of regular voters would have been about 1 in 2, compared to just 1 in 8 for citizens born between 1966 and 1975, and a mere 1 in 20 for those born between 1976 and 1982.

The impact of being able to identify regular voters via these computerized lists is likely to be cumulative over time. Older citizens get their participatory habits reinforced because campaigns continually ask them for their votes, whereas many younger citizens never get into the habit of voting because campaigns consider contacting them to be a poor investment of resources. The result is a classic "catch-22" situation—many younger people won't vote until a campaign mobilizes them, but many campaigns won't focus on them because they haven't established a history of voting participation. Such an effect is most likely to be seen in

TABLE 4.5
Percent Voting in All Three Major Elections From 2000 to 2003 in Los Angeles, San Francisco, and Orange County, California, by Age

	18–24	25–34	35–44	45–54	55–64	65–79	80+
PERCENT OF THOSE WHO WERE REGISTERED WHO ACTUALLY VOTED IN ALL THREE ELECTIONS	14	25	40	50	56	60	47
PERCENT OF CITIZENS REGISTERED ACCORDING TO CENSUS SURVEY	43	59	67	72	76	79	75
ESTIMATED PERCENT OF CITIZENS WHO VOTED IN ALL THREE ELECTIONS	6	15	27	36	43	47	35

Note: Age is as of the 2000 election.

Sources: Voter registration records of Los Angeles, San Francisco, and Orange County; 2002 Census Bureau Survey.

second-order elections over time, as these are the types of elections for which many people need a bit of a push before they will participate.

There are two types of American second-order elections for which time series turnout data can be examined—midterm elections and presidential primary elections. Table 4.6 presents data from the Census Bureau studies of midterm elections from 1966 to 2002. The patterns are much the same as found for presidential elections (see Table 4.1), except they are more pronounced. Despite starting from a substantially lower level in the mid-1960s, electoral participation by the youngest groups has fallen off even more sharply in midterm elections. The turnout rates of both the 21-to-24- and 25-to-34-year-old categories almost halved between 1966 and 2002. With seniors voting at slightly greater

TABLE 4.6

Turnout by Age in Midterm Elections, 1966–2002

	18–20	21–24	25–34	35–44	45–54	55–64	65+	65+/21–24 RATIO
1966	—	32	46	60	64	65	56	1.8 : 1
1970	—	30	41	50	58	64	57	1.9 : 1
1974	21	26	37	49	56	58	55	2.1 : 1
1978	20	26	38	50	56	61	56	2.2 : 1
1982	20	28	40	52	60	64	60	2.1 : 1
1986	19	24	35	49	55	63	60	2.5 : 1
1990	18	22	34	48	53	59	60	2.7 : 1
1994	17	22	32	46	55	59	61	2.8 : 1
1998	14	20	28	41	51	58	60	3.0 : 1
2002	15	19	27	40	50	57	61	3.2 : 1

Source: U.S. Census Bureau surveys.

levels than in past midterm elections, the generational gap grew to stunning levels.

Many observers thought that Al Qaeda's attack on American soil and the ongoing war against terrorism would reinvigorate electoral participation in America, especially among the young. But just over a year after the events of September 11 and as America prepared for an invasion of Iraq, less than one out of five Americans under the age of 25 bothered to vote, compared to three out of five people over the age of 65. It has long been said that old men send young men off to die in wars. What this has commonly referred to in a democracy is that older politicians who have worked their way up to high-level political offices are usually the ones who make these life-and-death decisions. But in the case of the first post-9/11 American national election, there was a deeper meaning evident, as it was older Americans who dominated the process of choosing the nation's Congress in 2002.

Ironically, it was young people's dissatisfaction with their lack of say toward American policy regarding the Vietnam War that provided the impetus for a major expansion of second-order election opportunities in the United States. Presidential primaries were adopted by many states after young antiwar Americans found their voices muffled in 1968 due to undemocratic procedures commonly used at that time to select national convention delegates. As can be seen in the data displayed in Table 4.7, the participation gap between young and old in presidential primaries during the 1970s was roughly the same as could be found in general elections. However, since then, age has become far more related to primary turnout, as young people's participation rate in primaries has stayed about the same, whereas older people have become substantially more likely to turn out to choose the presidential nominees. The 2000 National Annenberg Election Study found that 62 percent of senior citizens reported voting in their state's presidential primary, compared to just 18 percent among respondents less than 30 years of age.

TABLE 4.7
Turnout in Presidential Primaries/Caucuses by Age, 1972–2000

	18–29	30–44	45–64	65+	OLDEST/YOUNGEST RATIO
1972	17	23	28	28	1.6 : 1
1976	20	27	31	25	1.3 : 1
1980	15	26	38	38	2.5 : 1
1988	18	36	44	47	2.6 : 1
1992	13	31	41	41	3.2 : 1
2000	18	37	54	62	3.4 : 1

Sources: 1972–1992 American National Election Study; 2000 National Annenberg Election Study.

If it is fair to generalize that young Americans mostly yawn when given the opportunity to participate in midterm congressional elections and presidential primaries, then one can say that most are fast asleep when it comes to local elections. Localities are the basic building blocks of American democracy, and decisions made by local government are arguably the most relevant to citizens' day-to-day lives in America's relatively decentralized political system. Yet, due to the dearth of media attention on local politics, the vast majority of Americans do not participate in elections that are limited to just their own communities. Young people, because they are more mobile and often have less in the way of roots in the community, are particularly unlikely to be aware of local issues, and hence are relatively uninvolved in local politics.

One especially telling example of this pattern can be found in some 2003 participation data posted on the Internet by the town clerk of Concord, Massachusetts. One of the historic sites of the American Revolution, Concord continues to follow the traditional New England style of local participatory democracy. Just like in the Revolutionary period, Concord continues to hold regular town meetings where everyone can have a say about the issues facing the town and can vote on specific motions. In addition, there are regular elections for positions in the town's government and occasionally to decide referendum issues. Concord's town clerk reported election participation by age group throughout 2003, as well as the actual number of citizens in each age category who were known to be living there (whether registered to vote or not). The results for two town meetings and three town elections held during 2003 are displayed in Table 4.8. From these data, it is clear that one answer to the question of "Who runs Concord?" is that older people do, with ratios of participation between the oldest and

TABLE 4.8

Who Runs Concord? Turnout by Age in 2003

	18–29	30–39	40–49	50–59	60–69	70+	OLDEST/ YOUNGEST RATIO
TOWN ELECTION MAY 2003	6	23	40	36	51	43	7.2 : 1
TOWN ELECTION SEPTEMBER 2003	5	20	37	35	48	42	8.4 : 1
TOWN ELECTION MARCH 2003	4	12	22	25	36	34	8.5 : 1
TOWN MEETING AUGUST 2003	1	3	7	8	11	9	9.0 : 1
TOWN MEETING APRIL 2003	1	8	14	13	16	12	12.0 : 1

Source: Clerk of Concord, MA, official registration and turnout statistics.

youngest groups regularly exceeding 8 to 1. Of course, this is not due to any conspiracy to deny younger adults the rights that 18th-century citizens of Concord fought for. Rather, it is simply due to 21st-century American youths' neglect of local government.

THE TURNOUT GAP IN SECOND-ORDER ELECTIONS IN OTHER ESTABLISHED DEMOCRACIES

The pattern of seniors substantially outvoting young adults in second-order elections is hardly unique to American politics. Table 4.9 presents turnout data by age for a variety of regional and local elections around the world for which I have been able to find either survey data or official reports of participation by age. In Great Britain, a key part of New Labour's program for governing after they came to power in 1997 was their policy of

TABLE 4.9
Turnout in Various Regional and Local Elections Around the World by Age

	18–24	25–34	35–44	45–54	55–64	65+	OLDEST/ YOUNGEST RATIO
SCOTTISH ASSEMBLY, 2003	42	41	51	59	66	75	1.8 : 1
WELSH ASSEMBLY, 1999	36	39	52	67	70	72	2.0 : 1
LONDON MAYOR, 2000	27	37	51	57	58	62	2.3 : 1
BRITISH COLUMBIA PROVINCIAL, 2001	27	39	54	63	69	71	2.6 : 1
WESTERN AUSTRALIA LOCAL, 2003*	19	20	29	36	47	55	2.9 : 1
CHRISTCHURCH, NZ, CITY COUNCIL, 2001	20	30	45	62	75	89	4.5 : 1
	18–25	26–29	30–39	40–49	50–59	60+	
NORWEGIAN MUNICIPAL, 2003*	18	19	30	40	43	45	2.5 : 1

*Validated records of actual participation used here.

Sources: Christchurch: http://www.ccc.govt.nz/Elections/VotingAndNonVotingIn ChristchurchCity_October2001.pdf; British Columbia: http://www.elections.bc.ca/eac/ 2001VPStats_Summary.pdf; 2000 MORI Survey of London for UK Electoral Commission; 1999 Welsh National Assembly Election Study; 2003 Scottish National Assembly Election Study; Western Australian Electoral Commission; Statistics Norway: http://statbank.ssb.no/ statistikkbanken/Default_FR.asp?tilside=selecttable/hovedtabellHjem.asp& KortnavnWeb=kommvalg&PLanguage=1&nvl=true&direkte=1&PXSid=0.

devolution—that is, passing some powers from the national government to newly formed local political institutions. Because devolution created new electoral opportunities, it cannot be said that the elderly were more likely to vote just out of habit. Nevertheless, senior citizens were roughly twice as likely to vote in elections for the new Scottish and Welsh parliaments, as well as for London's first-ever mayoral election, than adults under the age of 25. A similar pattern of participation by age can be found in British

Columbia, Canada, where provincial elections have long been very important, given the fact that Canadian provinces have retained power over many policy arenas that are the purview of Britain's national government. On the other side of the Pacific, the 2001 election for the city council of Christchurch, New Zealand, had an even stronger age bias, with the oldest age category being 4.5 times more likely to vote than the youngest group. And even though Norway is about as far away as one can get geographically from the South Island of New Zealand, the participation of young people in the 2003 Norwegian municipal elections was similarly disappointing.

The data from Western Australia's local elections in 2003 merit special attention. Unlike the case for federal elections in Australia, for which participation is compulsory, Western Australians are free to choose whether or not to vote in local elections.[67] It might be hypothesized that because young Australians have had the experience of regularly going to the polls for national elections (which occur at least once every three years in Australia), they should be more likely to vote in local elections than young people elsewhere. The fact that Western Australia conducts its local elections entirely by mail should further facilitate the participation of young adults, making it possible for them to vote without having to take time off from work or school. Nevertheless, when the Western Australian Electoral Commission examined the records of who sent in their ballots in 2003, it found that less than 20 percent of people under the age of 35 did so, as compared to 55 percent of senior citizens.[68] Apparently, the act of voting in first-order elections does not necessarily establish a habit of voting that predisposes young adults to vote in second-order elections.

Finally, the question remains as to whether, like in the United States, generational differences in participation in second-order elections have widened in most established democracies. The best data for examining this question are from elections for the European Parliament. Although European parliamentary elections may seem to loom larger than national elections in that they involve voters from numerous countries all going to the polls at about the same time, they nevertheless have all the characteristics of a second-order election. Far less media attention is paid to these elections than national parliamentary elections, and the general feeling is that less is at stake. As a result, public information about European elections is shockingly low. For example, when a sample of European Union citizens was asked in 2002 whether "members of the European Parliament are elected by citizens like you and me," only 43 percent correctly answered that this was a true statement.[69] With such a lack of knowledge about these elections, it should not be surprising that fewer people vote in them compared to national parliamentary elections in the same countries, befitting their classification as second-order elections. And as the novelty of European parliamentary elections has worn off since they were first held in 1979, turnout in them has fallen off substantially.[70]

A comparison of turnout figures by age in the European parliamentary elections of 1979 and 1999 reveals that young Europeans have contributed disproportionately to turnout decline in these elections.[71] Table 4.10 presents turnout data from all the countries that participated in both elections, except for Belgium, which practices compulsory voting and hence has no turnout problems. In six of the seven countries, the ratio of participation between the oldest and youngest groups increased between 1979 and 1999. Countries such as France, Great Britain, and the Netherlands, which had some age disparity in European election turnout in 1979, had greater disparities 20 years later. And countries that

TABLE 4.10

Percent Reporting Casting a Ballot by Age Categories for the European Parliament, 1979 and 1999

	18–29	30–44	45–64	65+	OLDEST/YOUNGEST RATIO
FRANCE 1979	46	69	71	73	1.6 : 1
FRANCE 1999	42	51	67	72	1.7 : 1
NETHERLANDS 1979	59	67	78	77	1.3 : 1
NETHERLANDS 1999	42	44	56	70	1.7 : 1
WEST GERMANY 1979	69	74	71	67	1.0 : 1
WEST GERMANY 1999	40	54	61	59	1.5 : 1
ITALY 1979	94	96	97	95	1.0 : 1
ITALY 1999	79	84	84	81	1.0 : 1
DENMARK 1979	62	68	74	69	1.1 : 1
DENMARK 1999	57	69	79	72	1.3 : 1
IRELAND 1979	71	80	87	79	1.1 : 1
IRELAND 1999	39	70	83	72	1.8 : 1
GREAT BRITAIN 1979	41	51	62	63	1.5 : 1
GREAT BRITAIN 1999	18	27	37	50	2.8 : 1

Source: Eurobarometers, 1979 and 1999.

had roughly equal turnout rates by age in the first European parliamentary elections, such as West Germany, Denmark, and Ireland, had substantial differences by 1999. Only Italy did not have a problem in getting adults under the age of 30 to the polls for the 1999 European parliamentary elections. The case of Italy can best be interpreted as demonstrating once again that when turnout is very high in a society, young adults are swept along to the polls like everyone else. But once turnout drops, as so often happens in second-order elections, young people are then the most likely to be left on the political sidelines.

CONCLUSION: WAS LOWERING THE VOTING AGE A MISTAKE?

Considering how little use young adults have made of the voting franchise in recent years, some might consider the action of lowering the voting age to 18 in most established democracies to have been a mistake. This point of view is well expressed by political scientist Mark Franklin, who writes that:

> *With the benefit of hindsight, this reform was a really bad idea. It turns out that the well-intentioned decision to enfranchise young adults one election earlier than previously had the unanticipated consequence of giving rise to a lifetime of disenfranchisement for many of the intended beneficiaries. Ironically, almost any other age from fifteen to twenty-five would be a better age for individuals to first be confronted with the need to acquire the skills and knowledge necessary for casting a vote.*[72]

Franklin's argument here is based on the quite sensible premise that both voting and nonvoting are habits, and that if someone doesn't participate in his or her first election, then a lifetime habit of nonvoting may well be the result.

Though this theory regarding turnout decline seems sound at first glance, it doesn't hold up too well empirically. A number of findings presented in this chapter indicate that it would be a mistake to blame the recent decline of turnout in many countries on the lowering of the voting age. The cross-national data do *not* support the notion of an immutable life-cycle effect in which the turnout of newly enfranchised voters will necessarily be rather low. Indeed, in the early 1970s most countries had no real problem in getting young people to vote—even after many countries had lowered the voting age to 18. And the only established democracy that still does not allow 18- and 19-year-olds to vote—Japan—has nevertheless seen turnout decline sharply and a wide generation gap in electoral participation develop.

The central reason that so many of today's young adults fail to vote is not the age they are at but rather their lack of exposure to politics. Mark Franklin is certainly right to point to the problem of a lack of political skills among newly eligible voters in recent years. However, the data presented in previous chapters of this book indicate that this has not always been the case—including when most countries lowered the voting age. No one at that time could have foreseen that young adults in the 21st century would have such low levels of newspaper reading, TV news watching, or political knowledge.

Such trends lead me to be very skeptical regarding the current reform proposed in some circles to further lower the voting age to 16.[73] Based on an analysis of survey data from the European Social Survey, which includes 16- and 17-year-olds, this age group is even less likely to follow political news than people just a few years older.[74] Of course, if young people were given the franchise and required by high school teachers to follow politics as part of their classwork, this state of affairs could well change. But it seems risky to count on such assignments having a long-term impact on the media habits of young people.

It would perhaps be more likely for teachers to instill a stronger sense of the civic duty to vote if young people were confronted with the task of voting while they were in high school. Whether or not the voting age is lowered, this is certainly a goal that teachers need to address, as the data in the following chapter demonstrate.

CHAPTER 5

Do Young Adults See Voting as a Civic Duty?

The 2012 American National Election Study found that people under the age of 30 were the most likely to feel that voting is a choice rather than a duty. Of young people, 59 percent said voting is a choice as compared to 30 percent who said it is a duty. The views of senior citizens on this question were almost a mirror image of young people's views, with seniors being about twice as likely to say that voting is a duty rather than a choice.

Besides caring about who wins, another common reason political scientists have found for why some people vote is that they believe it is their civic duty. As Angus Campbell et al. wrote in their classic 1960 book *The American Voter*, "Wide currency in American society is given the idea that the individual has a civic responsibility to vote. When this norm becomes a part of the value system of the individual, as it has for most of our citizens, it may be regarded as a force acting directly on the turnout decision."[75] Andre Blais goes even further, arguing that many people who feel a duty to vote do so out of a sense of moral obligation. He writes, "To use a religious analogy, not voting can be construed as a venial sin: it is a wrong, one that weak human beings should be urged not to commit but may be forgiven for if they indulge in it."[76]

How one's sense of civic duty can influence the decision whether to vote or not was driven home to me in a very personal way in November 1998. I must confess that I did not vote in that election. Like many fellow baby boomers, I was relatively nonchalant about failing to participate. In my own mind, I felt that I had a pretty good excuse: About a week before the election, my father had undergone heart bypass surgery. I had flown across the country on short notice to be there, and the thought of getting an absentee ballot before I left California was not something that crossed my mind. (By the time I arrived on the East Coast, it was too late to request an absentee ballot by mail, but I later realized that I could have requested one in person just before I had left.) Ironically, I was able to keep a few commitments on election day to do radio interviews on the topic of nonvoting by simply e-mailing the producers that I would be at a different phone number. The fact that I wasn't voting that day came up a couple times on the air and led to some interesting discussions, but no real embarrassment on my part.

My father, by contrast, took a very different view regarding not voting. He had just gotten out of the hospital a couple days before election day and had scarcely been able to walk 10 yards outside the house, but nevertheless he said on Tuesday morning that he wanted to be driven to the polls. This idea did not sound wise to me under the circumstances. I proposed an alternative: given that my parents were clearly going to vote for different candidates for governor, I suggested that neither one vote, rather than go to the trouble of canceling out one another. This suggestion met with sharp resistance from my mother, who reminded me that there were many offices on the ballot besides governor and that they might actually agree on some of them. Most importantly, both my parents said that they considered it their duty as citizens to vote. My father pointedly remarked that voting was something that people who are alive are supposed to do, and having just survived a difficult, major surgery, he was absolutely determined to act as one who is alive. Facing such adamant demands, I felt little choice but to find some way to get my parents to the polls, and indeed went to more trouble to ensure that they voted than I would to cast a ballot myself.[77]

My parents' insistence that they really wanted to vote, my casual baby boomer attitude toward voting, and the outright political apathy I frequently see among today's college students are apparently all representative of current generational attitudes regarding the duty to vote. The goal of this chapter is to flesh out how these generational differences have emerged, both in the United States and in other established democracies.

HAVE YOUNG AMERICANS BECOME LESS LIKELY TO VIEW VOTING AS A DUTY?

Campbell et al. called voting a "responsibility" and Blais termed it an "obligation." To what extent do young people in the United States agree with such views? A 2002 CIRCLE survey of 1,200 Americans between the ages of 15 and 25 provides some insight. This survey posed the following question: "In your mind, which word best describes how you feel about voting: a right, a responsibility, a choice, or a duty?" Twenty percent responded that they considered voting a responsibility, and 9 percent said they felt it was a duty. Thus, fewer than one out of three young Americans expressed a view of voting as a civic obligation. On the other side of the coin, 34 percent responded that voting was a choice and another 31 percent called it a right.[78] It would be reading too much into such responses to say that these two-thirds of young Americans didn't value voting; they could well have seen voting as a fundamental right or a crucial choice. Nevertheless, without a strong sense that electoral participation is a responsibility and a duty for everyone, it seems reasonable to conclude that many of these young adults will not vote on a regular basis.

Whether young people are currently less likely than older adults to view voting as a civic duty remains to be established. Unfortunately, CIRCLE's interesting question has not been posed to a national sample of all ages. The best questions I'm aware of in any survey on the topic of voting as a civic duty are two that were asked by the Pew Research Center in their June 2000 and August 2003 surveys. Over 8,500 randomly selected individuals were asked whether they agreed with the statements "I feel it's my duty as a citizen to always vote" and "I feel guilty when I don't get a chance to vote." Overall, 63 percent completely agreed with the notion that it is one's duty to vote—roughly the same percentage of citizens who voted in 2004. And 37 percent said they feel guilty if they don't vote—roughly the same percentage of people who voted in the midterm election of 1998 that my father was so determined to participate in. As can be seen in the data displayed in Table 5.1, senior citizens were 1.7 times more likely than people under the age of 30 to completely agree that it is one's duty to vote, and 1.8 times as likely to say they feel guilty if they don't vote.

It might be argued that such age patterns are nothing to worry about, because one's sense of civic responsibility will increase as one grows older. Indeed, Andre Blais writes that "people are more likely to construe voting as a citizen duty as they grow older. On the one hand, their sense of attachment to their community

TABLE 5.1

Percent Completely Agreeing in Recent Years with Statements
Regarding the Duty to Vote

	18–29	30–44	45–64	65+
"I FEEL IT'S MY DUTY AS A CITIZEN TO ALWAYS VOTE."	44	61	71	75
"I FEEL GUILTY WHEN I DON'T GET A CHANCE TO VOTE."	24	34	44	44

Source: June 2000 and August 2003 Pew Research Center surveys.

increases, which makes them more inclined to think about duties toward the community. On the other hand, they have more exposure to the dominant norm that the good citizen ought to vote."[79] Although the factors that Blais lists seem sensible, he offers no supporting data; we should thus not presume that his hunch is correct, especially considering that some countervailing factors can also be hypothesized. Firstly, the concept of voting as a civic duty is taught in school, and lessons learned in school may be gradually forgotten if they don't prove relevant in later life. Many people quickly forget the algebra and chemistry they learned; why wouldn't they also forget concepts from civics courses? Secondly, as Americans grow older they are likely to see that many of their friends, relatives, and neighbors don't vote and that the political system continues to thrive anyway. Such life experiences may well lead some people to question whether it really is one's duty to vote.

The landmark socialization study of the high school class of 1965 and their parents provides some telling data indicating that students were substantially more likely than their parents to mention participation in politics as one of the most important qualities of good citizenship. Jennings and Niemi noted this difference and attributed it to "years of repetitive schoolroom exhortation to participate" that the high school students had received.[80] In their follow-up study, based on reinterviews eight years later, the impact of these exhortations was found to have worn off considerably, leading Jennings and Niemi to note that "As one enters the adult world, the difficulty of living up to these prescriptions becomes more obvious."[81]

Since the original 1965–1973 panel study, both generations were reinterviewed for a third time in 1982, and, incredibly, many respondents from the class of 1965 participated in a fourth interview in 1997.[82] One can hardly imagine a better source of data to test a life-cycle hypothesis than these interviews with the same individuals over so many years. Table 5.2 traces the frequency over time with which those interviewed mentioned political participation as an important attribute of a good citizen. Rather than a life cycle, the data mostly point to the stability of such attitudes over one's lifetime. Once the immediate effects of their schooling had worn off, there was relatively little change evident in the younger generation's responses between the ages of 25 and 50. Moreover, their parents' responses were similar in

---

TABLE 5.2

Percent of Panel Respondents Who Mentioned Political Participation as an Important Attribute of a Good Citizen, 1965–1997

	1965	1973	1982	1997
CLASS OF 1965 HIGH SCHOOL SENIORS	70	57	54	52
PARENTS OF THE CLASS OF 1965	48	40	44	—

Question wording: "People have different ideas about what being a good citizen means. Tell me how you would describe a good citizen in this country—that is, what things about a person are most important in showing that he is a good citizen?" Up to four responses coded. Codes 20 through 29 were counted as involving political participation.

Source: Youth–Parent Socialization Panel Study.

all three waves, with feelings of civic duty consistently being somewhat less salient for them than for their offspring.

Because feelings of civic duty are apparently established early in one's adult life and remain fairly stable afterward, it is important to continually reexamine age patterns, as the entrance of new cohorts into the population may well change the overall picture. The limited time series data available from the American National Election Studies seem to indicate that the relationship between age and civic duty has indeed changed over the years. Over the course of five decades, these surveys have periodically asked respondents whether they agree or disagree with the following statement: "So many other people vote in the national elections that it doesn't matter much to me whether I vote or not." As can be seen in Table 5.3, in recent years it has been young Americans who have been the *least* likely to express a clear sense of civic duty by disagreeing with the statement. In contrast, in the 1972–1980 period there was no clear age pattern, and in the very early years of the election studies, the elderly were slightly less likely than other age groups to indicate that voting really did matter to them.

TABLE 5.3
Percent Expressing a Sense of Citizen Duty by Age in the United States, 1952–2002

	<30	30–44	45–64	65+	DIFFERENCE BETWEEN 65+ AND <30
1952–1960	91	92	90	85	−6
1972–1980	87	91	92	87	0
2000–2002	70	82	86	80	+10

Question wording: "So many other people vote in the national elections that it doesn't matter much to me whether I vote or not." Table entries represent the percentage who disagreed with the statement.

Source: 1952–2002, American National Election Studies.

In sum, the fact that today's young Americans are the least likely to view voting as a civic duty is troubling in a number of respects. Contrary to any notion of a life-cycle effect, it has not always been the case that young people possess the weakest sense of citizen duty with regard to voting. Rather, this is something new. Furthermore, panel data collected over time indicate that we cannot necessarily expect young people's attitudes on the duties of citizenship to change as they age.

Of course, such conclusions must be viewed with some caution, given that they are based on relatively limited data. Data from other countries regarding citizen duty provide crucial confirmation of these American findings.

Can Similar Trends Be Found in Other Democracies?

The scholars who designed the first major cross-national surveys were very concerned with the question of how people viewed the responsibilities of citizenship. The famous Civic Culture Study by Almond and Verba posed an open-ended question that asked respondents what obligations citizens owed their country. Similar questions (some open-ended and some closed-ended) were asked in the follow-up Participation and Political Equality Study a decade later.

Table 5.4 presents data regarding the frequency with which respondents of different age groups said that political participation was an important citizen duty. In the five countries where an open-ended question was asked, there were wide differences in terms of how likely people were to mention political participation. In West Germany and the United States, over a third of respondents spontaneously said something along the lines of voting, keeping

TABLE 5.4

Percent Saying that Political Participation Is a Very Important Citizen Obligation, 1959–1970

	<30	30–44	45–64	65+	DIFFERENCE BETWEEN 65+ AND <30
OPEN-ENDED QUESTION					
GREAT BRITAIN 1959	7	5	7	6	−1
WEST GERMANY 1959	39	35	33	35	−4
ITALY 1959	6	7	7	2	−4
USA 1960	44	43	37	30	−14
USA 1967	53	54	43	36	−17
JAPAN 1967	12	11	7	4	−8
CLOSED-ENDED QUESTION					
AUSTRIA 1967	73	63	57	47	−26
NETHERLANDS 1970	70	70	70	60	−10

Open-ended question wording: 1959 and 1960—"People speak of the obligations which they owe to their country. In your opinion what are the obligations which every man owes his country?"; USA 1967—"What do you think is the most important obligation a citizen has to his country?"; Japan 1967—"What are the most important duties of a citizen?"

Closed-ended question wording: Austria 1967—"Here is a list of duties that it may be necessary for citizens to perform for a nation to continue. Which do you think is most important: work hard, be active in politics, obey the laws, be informed about public problems?" (percent choosing be active in politics or be informed about public problems as one of their choices reported in the table); Netherlands 1970—"Do you think that a citizen should play a very active role in public life, or rather active, or do you think this is not necessary?" (percent saying very or rather reported in the table).

Sources: Civic Culture Study, 1959–1960; Participation and Political Equality Study, 1967–1970.

informed about politics, or expressing one's political views. In contrast, less than 10 percent said something along these lines in Great Britain, Italy, and Japan. (The most common responses in these countries were as follows: Great Britain—to do one's job right; Italy—to be moral and honest; Japan—to pay taxes.) Despite these disparities, the age patterns are consistent in all five countries, either with little difference between age categories or with young people being slightly more likely to mention political participation as an important citizen obligation.

More direct measures of the concept of political obligation can be found in some closed-ended questions that were asked in Austria in 1967 and the Netherlands in 1970. In Austria, the younger someone was, the more likely he or she was to choose either being active in politics or being informed about public problems from among a list of important citizen duties. And in the Netherlands, both young and middle-aged respondents were more likely than the elderly to think that citizens should play a rather active role in public life. Thus, both open-ended and closed-ended survey data indicate that young adults in established democracies had a relatively strong sense of citizen duty during the 1959–1970 era.

Recent survey data from a wide spectrum of countries reveal that young adults in the 21st century are very different in this respect. Table 5.5 displays data from 15 established democracies regarding the percentage within each age group who expressed a strong sense that it is a citizen's duty to vote. In all 15 countries, a clear relationship between age and feelings of citizen duty is readily apparent, with young adults being considerably less likely than their elders to say that voting is an extremely important quality of good citizenship.

Tellingly, the countries that have the biggest generation gaps in terms of turnout, such as Great Britain and Japan, generally also have the largest age differences in opinion regarding the duty to vote. The correlation between the two age-difference measures is fairly strong, .56 (p < .05). Thus, one of the reasons for the decline of youth turnout in so many established democracies is no doubt the relative lack among today's young people of a sense of a civic obligation to vote.

TABLE 5.5
Percentage of Respondents in Various Countries Expressing a Strong Sense that It Is a Citizen's Duty to Vote, Circa 2002

	18–29	30–44	45–64	65+	DIFFERENCE BETWEEN 65+ AND <30
FINLAND	24	35	51	63	+39
GREAT BRITAIN	23	29	45	59	+36
NEW ZEALAND	28	40	48	61	+33
CANADA	55	74	80	85	+30
JAPAN	32	44	64	61	+29
DENMARK	54	66	78	82	+28
NORWAY	37	51	49	60	+23
GERMANY	36	40	48	58	+22
IRELAND	35	44	53	57	+22
SWITZERLAND	30	31	37	49	+19
AUSTRIA	44	53	63	62	+18
NETHERLANDS	26	32	39	44	+18
SWEDEN	56	55	62	72	+16
FRANCE	51	51	67	65	+14
ITALY	30	41	48	42	+12

Question wording: Europe—"To be a good citizen, how important would you say it is for a person to vote in elections: 0 = extremely unimportant; 10 = extremely important" (percent responding 9 or 10 shown in the table); Japan—"Many people vote at elections, so it doesn't matter if I don't" (percent clearly disagreeing shown in the table); New Zealand—"It is a citizen's duty to vote" (percent strongly agreeing shown in the table); Canada—"It is every citizen's duty to vote in federal elections" (percent strongly agreeing shown in the table).

Sources: 2002–2003 European Social Survey; 2000 Japanese Social Survey; 2002 New Zealand Election Study; 2004 Canadian Election Study.

CONCLUSION: A WINDOW INTO THE FUTURE?

Besides providing insight into turnout problems in these countries, attitudes concerning civic duty among recent entrants into the electorate may well provide a window into the future. Because the current generation of young people has a relatively weak sense of citizen duty, its current poor turnout rates may well be a constant state of affairs throughout their lifetimes. A generation who is relatively unlikely to see voting as an important civic responsibility is one who may well have many of its members lost as voters for the rest of its duration.

Short of implementing compulsory voting, which we discuss in the final chapter, it is probably too late to convince people who have already entered early adulthood that it is their obligation as citizens to vote. But it is never too late to convince people that politics really matters. One way to do this is to illustrate that, by passing up opportunities to vote, they are ceding important decisions to others who have different values and interests. As will be seen in the next chapter, young people are indeed doing just that.

CHAPTER 6

Does Low Youth
Turnout Really Matter?

In 2015, Canada's largest newspaper ran an editorial entitled, "Dear young people: Not voting? No one cares." The newspaper noted that Canada's federal budget had been "craftily geared" by the government to appeal to specific groups, especially the elderly. But as the editorial put it, "Left off the gravy train are young people. Why? Because they are way less likely to cast a vote than older people are."

Source: *Globe and Mail*, April 24, 2015 (http://www. theglobeandmail.com/globe-debate/editorials/dear-young-people-cant-be-bothered-to-vote-no-one-cares/ article24101272, accessed October 1, 2015)

Although much research has been done on the topic of non-voting, there is a surprising lack of concern among scholars about its consequences. This is not to say that scholars don't care if everyone votes or not. Implicit in most studies of voter turnout is a generally accepted norm that in an ideal democracy, all adult citizens vote in all elections. The fact that most democracies fall far short of this ideal does not trouble many scholars because they judge the results of elections to be largely unbiased by who votes and who does not. Wolfinger and Rosenstone's classic book *Who Votes?* demonstrates that nonvoters are demographically different from voters but argues that "these demographic biases do not translate into discernible overrepresentation of particular policy constituencies."[83] Ruy Teixeira's excellent book on the decline of U.S. turnout asks the question "What if they gave an election and everybody came?" and arrives at the answer "Not much."[84] He also places much weight on the finding that demographic factors are not related to policy preferences closely enough to result in substantial differences in the political attitudes of voters and non-voters. More recently, Verba, Schlozman, and Brady say in their comprehensive review of participation in the United States that "our data support the conclusion that voters and non-voters do not seem to differ substantially in their attitudes on public policy issues."[85] In effect, these scholars have posed the question "Why worry about disappointing electoral participation rates given that there is little difference between voters and nonvoters in terms of political behavior?"

The answer of this book is that whenever young adults are substantially less likely to vote than their elders, the ideal of government of the people, by the people, and for the people is seriously compromised. Most importantly, a democratically elected government should be looking out *for* the interests of *all* the people. If politicians know that young people are far less likely to vote than the elderly, why should they care about young people?

Officeholders need to concern themselves with their *core constituency*—the people who put them in power in the first place, and whose support they'll need to get reelected. According to David Mayhew, most politicians place reelection as their highest goal, and in order to reach it they engage in advertising and credit claiming aimed at their primary constituency.[86] From the perspective of this book, this means that politicians will be more likely to do something that will earn them credit with the elderly than with young adults. Thus, if there is a choice between passing legislation to reduce either the costs of prescription drugs or college education, the reelection imperative will naturally bias politicians to focus their energies on the former.

As John Kingdon has shown, the process by which some problems more than others come to occupy the attention of governmental officials is an important key to understanding what the government actually does.[87] Part of that process involves rational calculations by politicians regarding who is likely to vote and who is not. If young adults don't vote, then the issues that most concern them will often fail to make it onto the political agenda.

This chapter demonstrates that the concerns of young adults are indeed quite distinct from those of their elders. These divergent concerns translate into differences on the ideological spectrum and on various policy issues. Furthermore, evidence from recent U.S. elections, as well as elections from other established democracies, indicates that *more young people voting would definitely make a difference because the youth vote often favors different candidates and parties.*

DOES POSITION IN THE LIFE CYCLE AFFECT POLICY POSITIONS?

Winston Churchill is said to have remarked that "Any man who is not a socialist at the age of 21 has no heart, and any man who is still a socialist at the age of 40 has no head." The first part of the quote can be taken as saying that it is easy to favor economic equality when one is a young adult in the process of getting educated, finding a job, and beginning a career. But the second part implies that the notion of equality of income for all looks far different once one is middle aged and established in an occupation. In short, what the quote illuminates is that where one stands on the issues of the day depends in part on where one stands in life. An individual's place in the life cycle plays an important role in determining the kind of personal experiences that seem relevant at any given point in time, which in turn affects one's political priorities and values.

A Pew Research Center survey from October 2004 allows us to quantify the degree to which age differences exist on a variety of experiences that may have some political relevance. The findings displayed in Table 6.1 largely confirm commonsense expectations but are nevertheless instructive. Young adults are by far the most likely to be facing the challenges of paying for a college education and finding a job. On the other side of the coin, they are the least likely to own a small business or trade stocks and bonds. These economic experiences (or lack thereof) should make young people more likely to support activist policies of governmental intervention in the economy and to be less supportive of a probusiness policy agenda. Additionally, young people have a notably different lifestyle from the elderly on three key aspects of the New Right agenda. They are: 1) less inclined to be a born-again or evangelical Christian; 2) more likely to have a friend, colleague, or family member who is gay; and 3) less likely to have a gun or rifle at home.

Based on these findings, one would expect that young adults in the United States should be substantially more liberal than older people. Because this expectation stems from young people's position in the life cycle, such a pattern should be consistent at various points in time. Yet, it should also be the case that as people

TABLE 6.1

Lifestyle Differences by Age (percent responding affirmatively)

	18–29	30–44	45–64	65+
DO YOU HAVE A FRIEND, COLLEAGUE, OR FAMILY MEMBER WHO IS CURRENTLY SERVING IN THE MILITARY, RESERVES, OR NATIONAL GUARD?	67	61	53	40
DO YOU HAPPEN TO HAVE ANY GUNS, RIFLES, OR PISTOLS IN YOUR HOME?	31	35	45	44
ARE YOU THE OWNER OF A SMALL BUSINESS?	6	22	18	9
DO YOU TRADE STOCKS OR BONDS IN THE STOCK MARKET?	14	36	40	27
OVER THE PAST 12 MONTHS, HAS THERE BEEN A TIME WHEN YOU OR SOMEONE IN YOUR HOUSEHOLD HAS BEEN WITHOUT A JOB AND LOOKING FOR WORK, OR NOT?	48	38	36	21
OVER THE PAST 12 MONTHS, HAS THERE BEEN A TIME WHEN YOU HAVE BEEN UNABLE TO AFFORD NECESSARY HEALTH CARE FOR YOURSELF OR A FAMILY MEMBER, OR NOT?	22	30	27	16
ARE YOU CURRENTLY PAYING FOR THE COSTS OF COLLEGE TUITION OR STUDENT LOANS FOR YOURSELF OR SOMEONE IN YOUR FAMILY?	44	30	23	9
DO YOU HAVE A FRIEND, COLLEAGUE, OR FAMILY MEMBER WHO IS GAY?	49	52	48	25
WOULD YOU DESCRIBE YOURSELF AS A "BORN AGAIN" OR EVANGELICAL CHRISTIAN, OR NOT?	29	32	34	37

Source: October 2004 Pew Research Center survey.

progress from young adulthood to middle age, they will turn more conservative. All of these expectations are confirmed by the 1972–2004 General Social Surveys data presented in Table 6.2. The data collected in the early 21st century reveal that among people born in the 1980s, there are substantially more liberals

TABLE 6.2

Cohort Analysis of Political Ideology, 1972–2004
[entries are % conservative – % liberal]

BORN IN:	2000–2004	1990s	1980s	1970s
1980s	–14			
1970s	+1	–5		
1960s	+11	+4	–1	
1950s	+9	+5	–4	–21
1940s	+13	+8	+5	–9
1930s	+24	+19	+16	+13
1920s	+17	+20	+18	+15
1910s		+18	+14	+14

Source: 1972–2004, General Social Surveys.

than conservatives, whereas just the opposite is the case among those born in the 1920s and 1930s.[88] Interestingly, the latter group grew up during the height of liberalism when New Deal policies advocated by Presidents Franklin Roosevelt and Harry Truman reshaped the nation. The fact that this generation of New Dealers is now a mainstay of conservatism supports the theory that people move away from liberalism as they age. Indeed, there is clear evidence of a rightward shift of opinion among all the cohorts whose ideology we can track for decades, starting from a relatively young age. Americans like myself born in the 1950s provide a perfect example: Children of the 1950s were clearly quite liberal in the 1970s; by the 1980s their liberalism had moderated; as of the 1990s they were more likely to be conservatives than liberals; and in the 21st century, their conservative tendencies have increased further.

To more fully understand why political conservatism increases with age, it is helpful to look at a wide range of specific issues. The 2000 National Annenberg Election Study is particularly useful for examining age differences on issues because it has such a large sample size (over 94,000) and because over the course of the year many issues were asked about. Table 6.3 displays data from this survey on a wide range of issues that elicited a clear generation gap. As expected, based on their economic stage in life, young people are the most supportive of government policies that will reduce income differences. Specifically, they are naturally more in favor of increased government spending on items such as education

TABLE 6.3
Age Differences on Public Policy Issues in 2000

	18–29	30–44	45–64	65+
LIBERAL	31	23	21	16
MODERATE	39	41	40	39
CONSERVATIVE	29	36	39	45
FAVOR GOVERNMENT POLICIES TO REDUCE INCOME DIFFERENCES	61	53	46	42
SPEND MORE MONEY ON MILITARY	35	42	54	65
SPEND MORE MONEY ON EDUCATION	81	74	62	53
SPEND MORE MONEY ON AID TO MOTHERS WITH YOUNG CHILDREN	59	49	43	43
SPEND MORE MONEY ON SOCIAL SECURITY	61	60	59	50
FAVOR INVESTING SOCIAL SECURITY IN STOCK MARKET	71	68	60	45
FAVOR SCHOOL VOUCHERS	44	40	35	30
FAVOR GAYS IN MILITARY	64	62	59	53
GOVERNMENT SHOULD DO MORE TO PROTECT THE ENVIRONMENT	77	69	62	59

Source: 2000 National Annenberg Election Study.

and aid to mothers with young children. But the biggest generational gap on spending priorities is on the military budget, with only about a third of young adults favoring more spending for American armed forces and weaponry compared to two-thirds of senior citizens. Young people thus seem to realize the trade-off between social services spending and defense spending, with a clear preference for the former. Interestingly, their preference for more social services applies even to something that most of them believe they will never benefit from—Social Security.

Young Americans do not reject every conservative idea out of hand, however. When it comes to President Bush's proposal to allow people to invest some of their Social Security contributions in the stock market, young adults are by far the most supportive age group. In addition, they are substantially more in favor of the conservative-backed proposal for school vouchers that would enable parents to receive public funds to send their children to private schools. What these two examples illustrate is that young people are the most open to new ideas, regardless of the ideas' ideological origins. Indeed, on two relatively new liberal ideas—gay rights and government action to protect the environment—young people are also the most in agreement.

Perhaps surprisingly, given that young adults bear the physical risks of waging war, their willingness to embrace new policy endeavors applies to foreign commitments of American military might as well. When asked whether we did the right thing going into Iraq, Pew Research Center surveys in 2003, 2004, and 2005 consistently found young adults to be more approving of the war than senior citizens were. It might be thought that such an age pattern is due to the unique circumstance of America's now living under the threat of terrorist attacks. Yet, as Table 6.4

TABLE 6.4
Percent Saying We Did the Right Thing Getting into Various Wars by Age Group

	18–29	30–44	45–64	65+
KOREA 1952	55	48	37	29
VIETNAM 1964	59	55	42	31
VIETNAM 1966	56	55	44	35
VIETNAM 1968	39	40	25	19
VIETNAM 1970	42	38	26	16
VIETNAM 1972	36	38	27	16
IRAQ JULY 2003	66	67	63	54
IRAQ SEPTEMBER 2004	59	56	53	42
IRAQ JULY 2005	55	53	47	37

Question wording: Korea—"Do you think we did the right thing in getting into the fighting in Korea two years ago or should we have stayed out?"; Vietnam—"Do you think we did the right thing in getting into the fighting in Vietnam or should we have stayed out?"; Iraq—"Do you think the U.S. made the right decision or the wrong decision in using military force against Iraq?"

Source: 1952–1972 American National Election Studies; 2003–2005 Pew Research Center surveys.

demonstrates, young people were also the most likely to say that we had done the right thing in getting into Korea and Vietnam.

Today, many antiwar activists yearn for the spirit of protest seen during the 1960s, when many of America's youth spoke up loud and clear in opposition to the Vietnam War. The lack of a very vocal opposition to the Iraq War among 21st-century youth is sometimes seen as yet another indicator of their seeming political apathy. These stereotypes are clearly exaggerated, however. The survey data from both eras reveal that young Americans supported the war more than their elders did. Ultimately, going to war in a democracy involves trusting the judgment of the country's leaders that the cause justifies the sacrifices. Just as young Americans are known to be more generally trusting of government, so are they also apparently more likely to say that their government is doing the right thing in going to war.

Once the Vietnam War turned unpopular overall, it was naturally the young people who turned out to demonstrate, as throughout world history taking to the barricades has been the province of youth. Should a future war turn equally unpopular, demanding sacrifices from the country that appear unjustified, then antiwar activities are likely to pick up again among young Americans. When George W. Bush ran for reelection in 2004, such a state of affairs did not exist, as evidenced by the fact that Democratic nominee John Kerry had voted for the war and continually said that the country needed to keep its troops in Iraq. Young people thus had many policy reasons for being more against President Bush than other age groups were in 2004, but the Iraq War was not prominent among them.

Is There a Generation Gap in American Voting Behavior?

From these various data, two hypotheses can be drawn concerning the types of candidates whom young Americans should be particularly inclined to support. First, because of their openness to new policy approaches, young Americans should be more susceptible to the appeals of third-party candidates. Second, given that their policy stands are generally more in line with liberal principles than are their elders', they should be more likely to have supported the Democrats in recent elections.

Having grown up with multiple choices in virtually every aspect of American life, today's young adults should be particularly likely to want more choices in the political arena. Young adults would hardly be content with having a choice between just

Coke and Pepsi given all the choices they have become accustomed to. The same is true for the choice between Democrats and Republicans. In the 2000 U.S. National Election Study, respondents were asked which of the following outcomes regarding political parties best represented what they would like to see happen: a continuation of the two-party system, elections in which candidates run as individuals without party labels, or the growth of one or more parties that could effectively challenge the Democrats and Republicans. People under the age of 30 were the least supportive of the political status quo, with only 28 percent saying they wanted to retain the current two-party system, as compared to 55 percent of senior citizens. Young adults were more in favor of both candidates running without party labels—as Ross Perot did in 1992—and the development of a viable third party.

Such attitudes have been regularly translated into votes for presidential candidates running outside the two-party system. As can be seen from Table 6.5, in every case where a significant independent or third-party candidate emerged, young voters were the most likely to cast their ballots for him. Notably, this age pattern

TABLE 6.5
Percent Voting for Prominent Independent/Third-Party Candidates for President, 1968–2000

	18–29	30–44	45–64	65+
GEORGE WALLACE 1968	15	11	12	8
JOHN ANDERSON 1980	16	11	8	3
ROSS PEROT 1992	28	19	17	12
ROSS PEROT 1996	14	11	7	5
RALPH NADER 2000	5	2	2	2

Sources: 1968, 1980, 1992, and 1996 National Election Studies; 2000 National Voter Exit Poll.

occurred regardless of the ideology of the insurgent contender. Young voters were the most supportive of liberals Ralph Nader and John Anderson, centrist Ross Perot, and conservative George Wallace alike. These results should not be taken as indicating that young adults in recent years have had no ideological anchoring. Rather, what is operative in each case is that young people have felt less tied to the *traditional* ideological choices. When conservative third-party candidates appear, they can expect to get disproportionate support from young conservatives, and liberal third-party candidates can expect to get disproportionate support from young liberals. Were more young people to turn out at the polls, it is likely that more prominent individuals would challenge the two-party system, knowing that more voters would be open to their appeals. Thus, the lack of young voters at the polls really does matter in that it helps perpetuate America's two-party system. Some will see this effect as a good thing, whereas others will see it as unfortunate; but everyone should agree that it is consequential.

The extraordinary closeness of the 2000 and 2004 presidential elections has made it clearer than ever before in recent memory that who votes can make a big difference. A variety of changes in group turnout rates in the key states of Florida in 2000 and Ohio in 2004 could have swung the outcome in favor of the Democrats in both cases. In particular, if more young people had voted, there is good reason to believe that George W. Bush would *not* have won. As can be seen from the exit poll data displayed in Table 6.6, only 40 percent of Floridians under the age of 30 cast their ballots for Bush in 2000 compared to 52 percent among senior citizens. Given the razor-thin margin of victory, it is readily apparent that if turnout rates among young people had been just slightly higher, Al Gore would have carried the state and hence won the White House. If turnout rates had been equal across generations, and if

TABLE 6.6
Percent Voting for George W. Bush by Age in Key States

	18–29	30–44	45–64	65+
2000 FLORIDA	40	51	49	52
2004 OHIO	42	52	52	58

Source: Voter News Service Exit Polls.

nonvoters had voted like actual participants of the same age,[89] Gore's share of the two-party vote would have been approximately 50.8 percent, thereby making a recount unnecessary. Four years later in the key state of Ohio, the generation gap was even greater, with 42 percent of the youngest voters supporting Bush compared to 58 percent of seniors. In this case, if all age groups had voted at the same rate, Bush's narrow 51.1 percent of the two-party vote would have been transformed into a dead heat, requiring a recount. In short, the low turnout rate of young adults in 2000 and 2004 really mattered, denying crucial votes to Al Gore and John Kerry that could have changed the course of history.

ARE THERE AGE GAPS IN IDEOLOGY AND VOTING BEHAVIOR IN OTHER COUNTRIES?

Further evidence that low turnout among young adults really makes a difference can be found by examining recent survey data from other established democracies. If, as Churchill said, socialism looks a lot better to young people, then there should be a relationship between age and ideology where socialist principles have long been instrumental in defining the ideological spectrum, such as in most of Europe. In addition, young people are more in tune with post-material concerns such as the environment, which have increasingly come to shape left-wing thought in many established democracies.[90] The data on average ideological self-placement by age group displayed in Table 6.7 confirm these expectations. In 16 of the 18 countries, young adults are substantially more likely to place themselves to the left than older people.

TABLE 6.7

Left–Right Positioning by Age in Established Democracies, Circa 2000

	<30	30–44	45–64	65+	DIFFERENCE BETWEEN 65+ AND <30
JAPAN	5.0	5.4	6.0	6.1	+1.1
GREAT BRITAIN	4.8	4.9	5.0	5.7	+0.9
IRELAND	5.2	5.5	5.8	6.1	+0.9
NEW ZEALAND	5.1	5.9	5.8	6.0	+0.9
AUSTRALIA	5.0	5.2	5.6	5.7	+0.7
CANADA	5.2	5.6	5.6	5.9	+0.7
SWITZERLAND	5.1	5.1	5.4	5.8	+0.7
USA	5.6	5.7	5.8	6.3	+0.7
FINLAND	5.7	5.6	5.8	6.2	+0.5
BELGIUM	5.1	5.1	5.4	5.5	+0.4
DENMARK	5.6	5.4	5.3	6.0	+0.4
FRANCE	4.7	4.6	5.1	5.1	+0.4
GERMANY	5.6	5.4	5.3	6.0	+0.4
NETHERLANDS	5.1	4.9	5.0	5.5	+0.4
NORWAY	5.5	5.4	5.7	5.9	+0.4
ITALY	5.4	5.3	5.2	5.7	+0.3
AUSTRIA	5.3	5.3	5.4	5.4	+0.1
SWEDEN	5.3	5.3	5.3	5.4	+0.1

Question wording: "In political matters, people talk of 'left' and 'right.' How would you place your views on this scale, generally speaking?" 1 = Left; 10 = Right.

Source: 1999–2001 World Values Study.

Interestingly, the countries that have the sharpest age differences on ideology are also where the turnout disparity between young and old is most pronounced. In other words, not only are young Japanese, British, Irish, and New Zealander adults particularly less likely to vote compared to their grandparents' generation, but they are also substantially less rightwing. Austrian, Swedish, and Italian youth, by contrast, are fairly similar to their elders in both turnout rates and ideology. The correlation between the two difference measures is a striking .72, far too great to be due to chance (p < .001).[91] Correlation does not necessarily imply causation, and there is no clear answer to the question of why these two phenomena are related. It may be that when young people feel differently from older people on the issues, the choices offered by the parties lack an appeal to the young. In contrast, where there are few ideological differences between generations, the same appeals can mobilize all age groups to go to the polls. In any event, the very existence of this relationship certainly implies that low youth turnout matters. In countries where young people's turnout rates are well below average, their views are not likely to be well represented at the polls by their elders who do vote.

Indeed, there are sizable age differences in voting behavior in these countries. Table 6.8 presents survey data on voting choices by age for the countries where there is a considerable generation gap in electoral participation. In order to streamline the presentation, only parties for which there was at least a five-percentage-point difference in support between the youngest and oldest voters are shown in the table. For example, voting for the British Labour Party in 2005 is not shown because there were only slight differences by age group, whereas young people were clearly more likely to vote for the Liberal Democrats and less inclined to support the

TABLE 6.8

Recent Differences in Voting Behavior by Age in Various Democracies

	<30	30–44	45–64	65+	DIFFERENCE BETWEEN 65+ AND <30
GREAT BRITAIN 2005 CONSERVATIVES	26	29	29	35	+9
GREAT BRITAIN 2005 LIBERAL DEMOCRATS	32	25	24	23	–9
CANADA 2004 LIBERALS	31	28	39	40	+9
CANADA 2004 CONSERVATIVES	23	35	30	40	+17
CANADA 2004 NEW DEMOCRATS	24	20	15	11	–13
CANADA 2004 BLOC QUEBECOIS	16	11	12	7	–9
CANADA 2004 GREENS	6	5	4	1	–5
JAPAN 2003 LDP	25	36	38	52	+27
JAPAN 2003 DEMOCRATIC PARTY	36	44	44	28	–8
JAPAN 2003 NEW KOMEITO	27	14	11	14	–13
SWITZERLAND 2003 RADICAL DEMOCRATS	12	11	16	20	+8
SWITZERLAND 2003 SOCIAL DEMOCRATS	27	37	32	21	–6
SWITZERLAND 2003 PEOPLE'S PARTY	18	19	23	29	+11
SWITZERLAND 2003 GREENS	16	8	6	2	–14
GERMANY 2002 CDU/CSU	32	33	31	39	+6
GERMANY 2002 GREENS	17	14	12	8	–9
FRANCE 2002 CHIRAC (RPR)	24	17	18	42	+18
FRANCE 2002 MAMERE (GREENS)	14	10	5	0	–14
NEW ZEALAND 2002 LABOUR	35	41	42	52	+17
NEW ZEALAND 2002 NZ FIRST	2	8	10	14	+12

(Continued)

TABLE 6.8 (Continued)

	<30	30–44	45–64	65+	DIFFERENCE BETWEEN 65+ AND <30
NEW ZEALAND 2002 ACT NZ	9	6	10	3	–6
NEW ZEALAND 2002 GREENS	17	12	5	3	–14
IRELAND 2002 FIANNA FAIL	35	46	51	49	+14
IRELAND 2002 FINE GAEL	17	17	21	26	+9
IRELAND 2002 GREENS	8	6	3	1	–7
IRELAND 2002 SINN FEIN	11	8	3	2	–9
NORWAY 2001 SOCIALIST LEFT	24	16	13	6	–18
NORWAY 2001 LABOR	15	20	25	27	+12
NORWAY 2001 CHRISTIAN PEOPLE'S	10	15	11	19	+9

Source: Comparative Study of Electoral Systems; 2004 Canadian Election Study; 2003 Waseda University Japanese Election Study.

Conservatives. In Canada, age differences are found across the partisan spectrum, with young people far less likely to support the two largest parties. Were more young Canadians to vote, it seems probable that the party system would be even more fragmented than it is at present, further increasing the pressure for some form of proportional representation.

The tendency of young voters to be more supportive of new parties is found in many countries besides Canada. In Norway, young voters are more likely to direct their votes to the relatively new Socialist Left Party rather than to the traditional left-wing choice of the Labor Party. In Ireland, Sinn Fein gets its votes primarily from the young, whereas the traditional parties of Fianna Fail and Fine Gael are more favored by older voters. Japan's longtime ruling party—the Liberal Democrats—depends greatly on gaining votes from older voters in order to stay in power, whereas the newer parties like the Democratic Party of Japan draw well among younger voters.[92] And in a variety of countries—Germany, Switzerland, France, Ireland, New Zealand, and Canada—the data in Table 6.8 show that the Greens do substantially better with young people than with older voters.

Many of these countries practice some form of proportional representation, thereby giving all parties that exceed a minimal threshold (e.g., at least 5 percent of the national vote) representation in parliament roughly equal to their vote share. However, the fact that young people are so much less likely to vote in these countries means that support for these new parties is under-represented at the polls. Who votes does make a difference in many established democracies, shaping the alternatives that are presented to the voters as well as affecting the outcome of elections.

CONCLUSION: A GOVERNMENT
FOR OLDER PEOPLE?

As I wrap up my discussion of low youth turnout with students in my American voting behavior class, I like to read them the following newspaper editorial that I found online:

When it comes to jobs and other issues as well, the manifestoes of the political parties devote surprisingly little space to policies targeting young people. Instead, their pledges are heavily weighted to the concerns of seniors, with this tendency extending to how the budget should be allocated as well.

Some of the responsibility for this situation lies with the younger generations themselves. The voter turnout rate among young people is abysmally low. In the last election, for example, the turnout rate for those in their early 20s was a mere 35 percent. In contrast, 80 percent of people in their 60s cast ballots. To politicians, it is clear which of these two groups demands closer attention and lip service.

If this situation continues, the bills for the nation's massive fiscal budget deficit and the dawdling progress in pension reform will be passed on to the younger generation. The low turnout rate among young voters may very well be viewed as tacit approval for this course of action by lawmakers. We believe that an increase in the ballots cast by those in their 20s would prompt a shift in the leanings of the nation's politicians.

The first step in this journey can begin with this election. We urge all young people of voting age to get out to the polls and exercise their right of choice with a close eye on the future.[93]

I then ask the students what newspaper they think published this editorial. The answers I get are always the usual suspects—that is, the most prominent U.S. newspapers. So when I tell them that this was published in the *Asahi Shimbun*—Japan's largest newspaper (which has an English-language version)—they tend to take special notice. Seeing such an article in a foreign newspaper helps drive home the point that the problem of low youth turnout is not a uniquely American one. The basic arguments made in this Japanese newspaper editorial could easily be made in a wide variety of established democracies around the world.

It has often been said that politics is about answering the question of "Who gets what, when, and how?" Based on the evidence presented in this book, young adults are not likely to figure prominently in the answer to the "who" part of the question.

As the *Asahi Shimbun* editorial points out, a significant aspect of the political bias in favor of the elderly involves the issues that make it onto the political agenda. How to take care of a rapidly aging population is dominating political discussion in many countries, whereas concerns regarding young people who face difficulties in starting careers and families often are shunted aside. As American journalist Jane Eisner writes, the generational differences in turnout explain "why the U.S. is a nation where poverty among the elderly was addressed by Medicare and Social Security decades ago, and poverty among children remains a persistent and shameful reality."[94]

The bias toward older people that results from turnout differences between age groups is certainly not intentional on anyone's part. Yet, that does not make it right. Nor does the fact that everyone gets older eventually make the situation any better. A democracy should always strive to ensure that the views of all eligible voters are represented. Young adults should find that the government listens to them when they are young, not decades later after their needs and views have changed. The danger inherent in the developments discussed in this book is that if these trends continue unabated, many established democracies will be heading toward "a government of older people, by older people, and for older people."

CHAPTER 7

A New Civic
Engagement Among
Young People?

In the 2014 General Social Survey, young people were the most likely to say that they had taken part in a demonstration at some point in their lives. Thirty-two percent of people under the age of 30 said they had demonstrated, as compared to 21 percent among people aged 30 to 64, and 18 percent among senior citizens.

Within the wide range of debate over the state of citizen engagement in the United States, the topic of turnout is only one element, albeit a very important one. Since the original publication of this book, some scholars have argued that although young people may not be showing up at the polls in high rates, they are participating at high levels in community affairs and politics. According to this line of thinking, there is a new kind of political participation that is more attractive to young people: a hands-on type of involvement requiring more effort than the simple act of casting a ballot.

The most detailed discussion of this argument to date can be found in the 2006 book by Cliff Zukin et al. entitled *A New Engagement? Political Participation, Civic Life, and the Changing American Citizen*. Zukin and his colleagues assert that American "citizens are participating in a different *mix* of activities from in the past, and that this is due largely to the process of generational replacement."[95] They argue that new forms of participation have emerged, which they label as "citizen engagement" and define as "organized voluntary activity focused on problem solving and helping others."[96] Zukin et al. do not go so far as to argue that citizen engagement by young people substitutes for voting, but they simply state that this broader mix of political participation is changing the nature of American politics.

Russell Dalton, my UC, Irvine colleague and sometimes coauthor, goes much further in his thought-provoking paper entitled "Citizenship Norms and Political Participation in America: The Good News Is … the Bad News Is Wrong." Dalton asserts that "if feelings of citizen duty are eroding among the young, this may be balanced by new norms of engaged citizenship."[97] He portrays voting as a placid, old-fashioned way of making one's opinions heard by the government. In Dalton's view, "if one is dissatisfied with the policies of the Bush (or Clinton) administration, waiting several years to vote in the next election as a means of political participation seems like political inaction."[98] In contrast, he argues that today's young adults have increasingly adopted direct forms of political action—protesting, boycotting, and Internet-based actions —that can have an immediate impact. Dalton incisively notes that "older people typically castigate the young for not being like them —this has been true since the time of Aristotle—and attribute negative political developments to the eroding values and poor behavior of the young."[99] In this respect, he maintains that young Americans need to be judged by the totality of their political participation, rather than the traditional standards of their elders. Dalton concludes that the overall picture of youth participation is a bright one.

Given the arguments made by Zukin et al. and Dalton, the central thesis of this book stands challenged as missing the forest by focusing on the trees. Although it was never my intention to present a comprehensive overview of political participation, in order to address this critique it now seems necessary to do so. Therefore, this chapter examines age patterns of political participation over time in a variety of forms. The overall outlook for participation of young people is generally not as bad as is the case with voting, but it is not a particularly rosy scenario either.

ARE TODAY'S YOUNG PEOPLE THE VOLUNTEER GENERATION?

The most frequently cited type of participation among today's youth involves taking part in volunteer work. As Harvard students Ganesh Sitaraman and Previn Warren write in *Invisible Citizens: Youth Politics After September 11*, "young people are some of the most active members of their communities and are devoting increasing amounts of their time to direct service work and voluntarism."[100] In *Democracy at Risk*, Stephen Macedo et al. take a detour from their usual focus on the erosion of civic life to single out volunteering as one important positive trend in citizen participation. They write that volunteering has been spurred in large part by "the proliferation of private and public programs designed to increase youth volunteering and public service."[101]

There are a variety of surveys that provide evidence regarding the increase of youth voluntarism in recent years. In my judgment,

FIGURE 7.1

Percent of High School Seniors Volunteering at Least Once a Month,
1976–2004

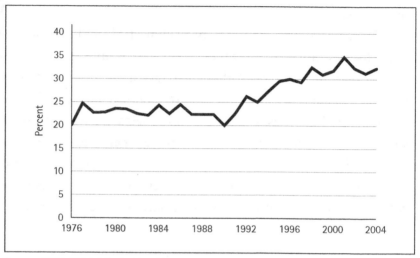

Source: 1976–2004, Monitoring the Future National Surveys.

the richest data source can be found in the national surveys of 12th
grade students conducted annually since the mid-1970s by the
Monitoring the Future project at the University of Michigan.
(Information on these studies can be found at http://www.
monitoringthefuture.org/.) Figure 7.1 charts the increase in the
percentage of high school seniors who said they volunteered in
their community at least once a month. In the 1970s and 1980s,
voluntarism was relatively steady, averaging about 23 percent.
Thereafter, regular participation in volunteer work increased
substantially. In 2004, an average of 33 percent of 12th graders
said they had volunteered on at least a monthly basis. As noted by
Macedo et al., this increase coincides with a series of presidential
initiatives: George H. W. Bush's Points of Light Foundation, Bill
Clinton's AmeriCorps and Corporation for National Service, and
George W. Bush's Freedom Corps and Citizen Corps.

There is no way to spin the increase in youth voluntarism in anything but a positive direction. This surge in youth voluntarism has led to a wealth of good work for a multitude of worthy causes. Young people have been encouraged by various programs to volunteer their time, and many of them have responded to this call to perform services for their communities.

As with any good deed, some kinds of people will respond much more readily than others. What types of youth have responded to this call and why? To ask this question is not to disparage voluntarism but to better understand it. When I first started talking to students in my classes about how their generation has been volunteering at a record rate, many of them commented that this trend can be better understood when placed in the context they grew up with. While not criticizing their peers who have volunteered, these students noted that many young people volunteer as a way of building up their résumés for their college applications. In other words, they've not only been taught that volunteering is a great way to do a good deed but also that it looks really good on their high school record. The crux of these comments from some of my undergraduates was that they wouldn't be surprised to find that most of the increase in volunteering could be traced to the most ambitious high school students.

In order to test this hypothesis, I further examined the volunteering patterns in the Monitoring the Future data, controlling for two variables: expectation of graduating from college and high school grade point average. The data displayed in Table 7.1 provide evidence that is consistent with my students' hypothesis. Among "A" students who said they definitely expected to graduate from college, volunteering at least once a month rose by 18 percent between the late 1970s and the early 21st century.

TABLE 7.1

Percent of High School Seniors Volunteering at Least Once a Month
by College Plans

	WILL DEFINITELY GRADUATE FROM COLLEGE BY GPA				WILL PROBABLY GRADUATE FROM COLLEGE	DO NOT EXPECT TO GRADUATE FROM COLLEGE
	A	A–	B+	B OR LESS		
1976–79	37	33	33	28	23	18
1980–89	36	31	29	25	22	18
1990–99	47	41	35	28	23	18
2000–04	55	45	37	31	27	20
CHANGE	+18	+12	+4	+3	+4	+2

Source: 1976–2004, Monitoring the Future National Surveys.

Similarly, regular voluntarism increased substantially—on the order of 12 percent—among "A-" students who were sure they would get a college degree. For all other groups of 12th-grade students, however, only marginal increases in community volunteering have occurred, ranging from 2 to 4 percent. Over time, these patterns do not necessarily prove that many of the brightest high school seniors have been motivated to volunteer for community work in order to bolster their college applications, but they are certainly compatible with such an explanation.

Of course, voluntarism among young people includes more than just participation in one's senior year of high school. Table 7.2 expands the analysis to cover all age groups in the United States at two points in time: 1989 (just before the push to increase volunteering started) and 2004. Although the phrasing of the question differed in these two Census Bureau studies, the concept of volunteering over the past year is a straightforward matter for which

TABLE 7.2
Percent Reporting Volunteer Work by Age Group in the U.S. and Western Europe

	15-18	19-23	24-29	30-39	40-49	50-59	60-69	70-79	80+
U.S. 1989	14	11	16	27	28	22	21	18	9
U.S. 2004	30	20	21	28	32	30	28	26	18
WESTERN EUROPE 2002/3	19	20	20	22	26	25	24	19	12

U.S. 1989 question wording: "Last week did you do any unpaid volunteer work?" (If no) "Even if you did not do any unpaid volunteer work last week, did you do any unpaid volunteer work over the past 12 months?"

U.S. 2004 question wording: "Since September 1st of last year, have you done any volunteer activities through or for an organization?"

European question wording: "For each of the voluntary organizations I will now mention, please use this card to tell me whether any of these things apply to you now or in the last 12 months." (Percent reporting "voluntary work" for one or more of the following organizations: sports/outdoor activity club, cultural/hobby activity, trade union, business/profession/farmer, consumer/auto, humanitarian, environment/peace/animal, religious/church, political party, science/education/teacher, social club, other voluntary organization.)

Sources: 1989 and 2004 U.S. Census Bureau Studies; 2002/3 European Social Surveys of Austria, Belgium, Denmark, Finland, France, Germany, Great Britain, Ireland, Italy, Netherlands, Norway, and Sweden.

question wording shouldn't matter much. For purposes of this analysis, we are more interested in how the pattern of volunteering by age has changed over time than in the precise percentages. A comparison of the age patterns in the two years leaves little doubt that volunteering has increased markedly among 15-to-18-year-olds in the United States. In 1989, this age group was one of the least likely age groups to have volunteered in the past year; by 2004, it ranked almost at the top.

One of the main reasons that analysts have widely applauded the increase in voluntarism among high school-aged youth is that lifelong habits are often established at this time of life. Even if many American teenagers volunteer just to bolster their college applications, it can nevertheless be argued that they learn about the positive impact volunteering makes and become socialized to continue such work throughout their lives. However, the data displayed in Table 7.2 for 19-to-23-year-olds and 24-to-29-year-olds provide relatively little support for such a development so far. In 2004, both of these age groups ranked near the bottom in terms of frequency of volunteering despite being part of a generation of young Americans who had positively responded to calls to volunteer while in high school. In short, young Americans are volunteering at record rates as they prepare for college, but after they reach this age, there is currently no sign of a great new spirit of voluntarism amongst this generation.

Perhaps this dip in volunteer work participation is just part of a natural life cycle, and these cohorts will eventually get back into their high school spirit of chipping in for their communities. If such a life cycle exists, then it ought to be apparent in data from other established democracies. Fortunately, the European Social Survey has started to ask about volunteer activity. Given that these national surveys do not have anything approaching the vast sample size of the U.S. Census Bureau surveys, I have combined data from 12 Western European democracies at the bottom of Table 7.2 in order to obtain a sufficiently large number of cases within each age category. The results indicate that volunteering increases slightly with age from the teenage years through middle age, declines a bit after age 50, and finally drops off markedly after age 80. There is no evidence of a natural dip in volunteering after leaving high school in either the aggregated European data or the individual country results (not shown in the table).

Given these results, we should not necessarily expect that America's youth will volunteer in substantially greater percentages once the incentive of building up one's résumé for college has passed. Perhaps the experience of volunteering that many of them had in high school will spur them to greater involvement in community affairs in the future. There is no sign of this happening yet, as will be seen in the next section.

HAVE YOUNG PEOPLE BECOME MORE INVOLVED IN COMMUNITY PROBLEM SOLVING AND CONTACTING GOVERNMENTAL OFFICIALS?

Even those scholars who believe that there is a vibrant new spirit of voluntarism among America's youth acknowledge that there is no guarantee that these inclinations will translate into activity in the political realm. Many types of volunteering—helping out at a place of worship, a senior citizen center, or a homeless shelter—have little direct political relevance. Do young people who get involved in these sorts of volunteer activities learn participatory skills that increase the likelihood that they will get involved in politics later in life? Perhaps one type of participation will help build a bridge that will carry young people over into participation in the political arena. However, if many young people believe that volunteering can be a more effective way of making a difference than participating in politics, then this scenario would appear doubtful. Thus, Sitaraman and Warren express concern with the response patterns they found in Harvard's Institute of Politics' 2000 survey of undergraduates: 85 percent of college students felt that "community voluntarism is better than political engagement for addressing issues facing the community."[102] Findings such as these led Macedo et al. to conclude that for many young Americans, volunteering is an alternative form of participation rather than a bridge to political action.[103]

On the other side of the fence, Zukin et al. argue that there is much *potential* for civic engagement to be linked to political engagement. Their initial investigation of the political relevance of voluntarism revealed that only 21 percent of volunteers nation-wide said they participated in order to address a social or political problem, as compared to 85 percent who said they did so in order to help others. However, Zukin et al. hypothesized that this portrait of voluntarism might change if people were asked more detailed questions about their possible political motivations. In a survey of New Jersey, they found that 44 percent of people who regularly volunteered connected this work to politics, either by viewing it as something that government should address or by having contacted a government official concerning it. In addition, over two-thirds of respondents who had participated in community problem solving said they considered this as an effort to address a social or political problem. Zukin et al. are appropriately cautious about these findings, noting they apply only to the minority of citizens who volunteer on a regular basis or work with others on community problems. Furthermore, they acknowl-edge uncovering no evidence that young respondents were more likely to make a connection between civic engagement and political participation.[104]

Zukin et al.'s analysis sets up the following fundamental question that they did not address but easily could have: "Has greater involvement in volunteer activities among young people made them more likely to work on community problems and contact governmental officials to express their views than previous generations?" The 2002 National Civic Engagement Surveys conducted by Zukin et al. also asked respondents about working with others to solve a community problem. Although their question differed from the questions asked in the 1967 and 1987 national surveys of participation, the concept is certainly the same. Table 7.3 compares the response patterns by age group in each of the three time periods. The trend is undeniably toward greater participation in community problem solving amongst all age groups. However, the basic relationship between age and taking part in community affairs has scarcely changed at all, as the increases are roughly the same for each age category. It is good news that so many more young adults were working on the problems of their communities in 2002 than in 1967, but young Americans are still bringing up the rear in this dimension of political participation.

The picture on contacting governmental officials is similar, though less positive with regard to young people. Table 7.4A compares the percentage of respondents within each age group

TABLE 7.3
Percent Taking Part in Community Problem Solving by Age, 1967–2002

	18–29	30–44	45–64	65+
1967	22	33	35	27
1987	22	36	41	32
2002	31	39	47	37
CHANGE	+9	+6	+12	+10

1967, 1987 question wording: "Have you ever worked with others in this community to try to solve some community problem?"

2002 question wording: "Have you ever worked together informally with someone or some group to solve a problem in the community where you live?"

Sources: 1967 Political Participation in America Study; 1987 General Social Survey; 2002 National Civic Engagement Surveys I and II.

TABLE 7.4A
Percent of Americans Who Have Ever Contacted a Political Official by Age Group, 1967–2004

	18–29	30–44	45–64	65+
1967	23	36	33	27
1987	28	47	47	37
2004	23	40	56	47
CHANGE	0	+4	+23	+20

Question wording: 1967 and 1987: "Have you ever personally gone to see, or spoken to, or written to some member of local government, or some other person of influence in the community about some need or problem? What about some representative or governmental official outside of the local community—on the county, state or national level? Have you ever contacted or written to such a person on some need or problem?" (Percent reporting yes to either question recorded in the table.)

2004: "Here are some different forms of political and social action that people can take. Please indicate, for each one, whether you have done any of these things in the past year, or whether you have done it in the more distant past—contacted, or attempted to contact, a politician or a civil servant to express your views."

Sources: 1967 Political Participation in America Study; 1987 General Social Survey; 2004 General Social Survey.

who said that they had contacted U.S. politicians or civil servants to express a viewpoint in 1967, 1987, and 2004. Although the 2004 question was quite different from the questions asked in previous studies, the concept of contacting officials is phrased similarly, and as with the earlier questions, people were asked to respond within the context of a long time frame. Because older respondents have had more lifetime opportunities to contact officials, the extended time frame in the wording of the question should naturally result in them being more likely to report having done so. Indeed, this is consistently the case. What is particularly noteworthy in these data, however, is that the participation gap between younger and older Americans has widened markedly. In 1967, people between the ages of 45 and 64 were only 10 percent more likely to say that they had contacted a public official than people under 30. In 2004, the difference between these two age

TABLE 7.4B

Percent of Europeans in Six Countries Who Have Contacted Public Officials, 1974 and 2004 Compared

	18–29	30–44	45–64	65+
1974	9	16	14	8
2004	14	25	32	25
CHANGE	+5	+9	+18	+17

Question wording: 1974: "How often do you contact public officials or politicians: often, sometimes, seldom, never?" (Percent responding "often" or "sometimes" reported in the table.)

2004: "Here are some different forms of political and social action that people can take. Please indicate, for each one, whether you have done any of these things in the past year, or whether you have done it in the more distant past—contacted, or attempted to contact, a politician or a civil servant to express your views."

Sources: 1974 Political Action Study and 2004 International Social Survey Program Studies of Great Britain, West Germany, Netherlands, Austria, Switzerland, and Finland.

groups had ballooned to 33 percent. As shown in the change figures at the bottom of Table 7.4A, the increase in contacting political elites in the United States over the last few decades can be traced almost entirely to greater participation among people over the age of 44.

A similar pattern of change over time can be found in the data from six European countries displayed in Table 7.4B. In 1974, there was a modest curvilinear relationship between age and the percentage of people contacting public officials. By 2004, the relationship had become much steeper as increases in contacting public officials were most prevalent amongst the older age categories. As in the United States, the survey evidence indicates that citizens have become more actively involved in politics by communicating their views directly to decision makers. This is a positive development, but the increased discrepancy between age groups on this important form of political participation does not augur well for equality of political representation across generations.

Have Young People Turned to
Unconventional Forms of Political
Participation?

Young people are almost always at the forefront of new types of activities and are typically more adventurous and open to novel ways of doing things. If there really is a new kind of political engagement, then it seems reasonable to hypothesize that young people would be among the first practitioners of new means of involvement in the political process. Contacting politicians and working within groups to address community problems might be considered old-fashioned ways of working within the confines of the political establishment by many young people. Therefore, they may prefer to focus their energies on unconventional forms of political participation that could directly challenge the established order. Protesting, petitioning, and boycotting are among the types of unconventional forms of participation that political scientists typically look at. All of these forms of political participation go beyond simply conveying one's views to authority figures. Their object is not just to make opinions heard by those in power but to change the status quo through means other than elections. It is primarily these sorts of activities that Russell Dalton has in mind when he writes about young people focusing on direct forms of political action that can have an immediate impact.

Have young Americans become more inclined to participate in such unconventional forms of political action in recent years? To answer this question, we can return to the Monitoring the Future surveys of high school seniors. Since 1976, these studies have asked students whether they have ever taken part in a variety of forms of political participation or planned to do so in their lives. The percentage who say that they have already participated in these activities before turning 18 is relatively low, but many more say they plan to do so. Because the trends for these two responses parallel one another, I have combined them in order to simplify the presentation. Table 7.5 presents the decade-by-decade results for five forms of political participation—three conventional and two unconventional activities. These data do not support the notion that young Americans have become more inclined to participate in unconventional forms of political action. The percentage of recent high school seniors who say they have demonstrated or boycotted, or plan to do so, is actually slightly below the comparable percentage in the late 1970s. On the other hand, these declines have been less steady and dramatic than young people's declining interest in conventional forms of participation, such as working on campaigns, making political contributions, and writing to public officials. In that sense, it can be said that unconventional political action has assumed a larger share of the pie of young Americans' expected political repertoire. But given that the size

TABLE 7.5

Percent of High School Seniors Who Have Ever Done, or Plan to Take Part in, Various Forms of Conventional and Unconventional Political Action, 1976–2004

| | CONVENTIONAL POLITICAL ACTION | | | UNCONVENTIONAL POLITICAL ACTION | |
	WRITE TO PUBLIC OFFICIALS	GIVE $ TO A POLITICAL CAMPAIGN OR CAUSE	WORK ON A POLITICAL CAMPAIGN	TAKE PART IN A LAWFUL DEMONSTRATION	TAKE PART IN A BOYCOTT
1976–79	37	24	19	21	29
1980–89	32	22	15	19	20
1990–99	29	16	11	24	28
2000–04	26	16	10	19	23
CHANGE	–11	–8	–9	–2	–6

Source: 1976–2004, Monitoring the Future National Surveys.

of the pie has been shrinking, this development can hardly be considered good news.

Another interpretation of these data takes into account that what scholars labeled as unconventional forms of political action in the 1960s and 1970s are now common practices that 21st-century youth view as standard forms of political participation. Thus, young people who are interested in politics now say they expect to participate in protests, boycotts, or petition drives simply because it is what they are accustomed to seeing politically active people do. Such a scenario was foreseen by Barnes and Kaase's path-breaking work on unconventional participation in the 1970s. They concluded that though such forms of participation were then relatively new, they were not a passing fad, but rather part of a trend that would become "increasingly apparent as the well-educated young march down the corridors of time."[105] A cohort analysis of the data from Barnes and Kaase's 1974 U.S. Political Action Survey and the 2004 U.S. General Social Survey bears out this prediction. As shown in Table 7.6A, age cohorts that can be compared over time appear to be relatively stable in terms of willingness to participate in petitioning, boycotting, and demonstrating. The change is that the cohorts who were most reluctant to participate in such activities in 1974 have mostly died and been replaced by young people who are just as inclined to participate in such actions as the generation that pioneered them in the 1960s. Back in 1974, young Americans were by far the most likely to have actually participated in petition drives, boycotts, and demonstrations. In 2004, all age cohorts born in the 1940s or later were taking part in them at roughly the same rate.

Comparable data from seven European democracies displayed in Table 7.6B reveal very similar age patterns of participation in these activities over the same three decades. In Europe during the

TABLE 7.6A
Cohort Analysis of Participation in Petitioning, Demonstrating, and Boycotting in the U.S.

BORN IN:	'80s	'70s	'60s	'50s	'40s	'30s	'20s	'10s	BEFORE 1910
1974 AVERAGE # OF "HAVE DONE" AND "MIGHT DO" RESPONSES	—	—	—	2.17	2.10	1.91	1.74	1.57	1.26
2004 AVERAGE # OF "HAVE DONE" AND "MIGHT DO" RESPONSES	2.48	2.30	2.24	2.26	2.23	2.05	1.67	—	—
1974 AVERAGE # OF "HAVE DONE IN LAST 10 YEARS" RESPONSES	—	—	—	.55	.56	.48	.42	.34	.27
2004 AVERAGE # OF "HAVE DONE IN LAST YEAR" RESPONSES	.69	.62	.71	.66	.72	.56	.46	—	—

Question wording: 1974: "Please place the cards on this scale to show whether: 1) you have actually done any of these things during the past 10 years; 2) you would do any of these things if it were important to you; 3) you might do it in a particular situation; or 4) you would never do it under any circumstances. Items listed—signing a petition; joining in boycotts; attending lawful demonstrations." 2004: "Here are some different forms of political and social action that people can take. Please indicate, for each one, whether: 1) you have done any of these things in the past year; 2) you have done it in the more distant past; 3) you have not done it but might do it; or 4) have not done it and would never, under any circumstances, do it. Items listed—signed a petition; boycotted, or deliberately bought, certain products for political, ethical or environmental reasons; took part in a demonstration."

Sources: 1974 Political Action Study; 2004 General Social Survey.

1970s, the younger one was the more likely to be involved in such actions. But by the 2000s, only Europeans who were socialized before the turbulence of the 1960s had gotten into the swing of such political activities. As in the United States, the addition of new generations that considered these actions to be a standard part of political action resulted in higher overall levels of participation. Although the 1970s question wording asked respondents if they

TABLE 7.6B

Cohort Analysis of Participation in Petitioning, Demonstrating, and Boycotting in Seven European Countries

BORN IN:	'80s	'70s	'60s	'50s	'40s	'30s	'20s	'10s	BEFORE 1910
1974 AVERAGE # OF "HAVE DONE IN LAST 10 YEARS" RESPONSES	—	—	—	.47	.47	.40	.37	.29	.23
2002–03 AVERAGE # OF "HAVE DONE IN LAST YEAR" RESPONSES	.57	.65	.65	.65	.60	.48	.32	—	—

Question wording: 1974: "Please place the cards on this scale to show whether: 1) you have actually done any of these things during the past 10 years; 2) you would do any of these things if it were important to you; 3) you might do it in a particular situation; or 4) you would never do it under any circumstances. Items listed—signing a petition; joining in boycotts; attending lawful demonstrations." 2002–03: "There are different ways of trying to improve things in [a country] or help prevent things from going wrong. During the last 12 months, have you done any of the following? Items listed—signed a petition, boycotted certain products, taken part in a lawful public demonstration."

Sources: 1974 Political Action Study and 2002–2003 European Social Surveys of Great Britain, Germany, Netherlands, Austria, Italy, Switzerland, and Finland.

had taken part in boycotts, demonstrations, and petition drives in the past decade whereas the more recent surveys asked if they had done them in just the last year, the average number of participatory responses nevertheless increased.

Are these increases in political action part of a new style of political engagement? I don't think the evidence supports such a conclusion. To call this a new style of political engagement is like calling rock a new kind of music. In both cases, innovations were pioneered by the baby boom generation and picked up by subsequent generations. Like rock music, which was once seen as anti-establishment but is now a well-accepted musical style, these new forms of political participation have become a standard part of an active citizen's political repertoire.

CONCLUSION: YOUNG PEOPLE'S PLACE IN THE FOREST OF POLITICAL PARTICIPATION

This examination of the forest of political participation leaves a different overall impression than simply looking at turnout rates. Although turnout rates have generally been going down in the United States and other established democracies, participation in non-electoral forms of politics, such as contacting public officials, working on community problems, protesting, boycotting, and signing petitions, has been going up. Furthermore, the ranking of the United States on many non-electoral forms of political participation is far higher than one might expect from its relatively low voter turnout rate. According to the recent Comparative Study of Electoral Systems, the United States had the highest level of citizens who had worked together with people to express their political views, and ranked 4th out of 18 on contacting public officials. Similarly, the 2004 International Social Survey Program found that U.S. respondents were the most likely to say they actively participated in a political party, and ranked 2nd out of 16 in joining Internet political forums, and 5th on signing petitions. In sum, my review of the various facets of political participation leads me to agree with Russell Dalton that there is plenty of good news to report.

But have young Americans been leading the way in these positive developments in civic participation? With the exception of volunteering among 15-to-18-year-olds, which is probably due to college-bound students trying to build up their résumés for college, there is little evidence of exceptional youth participation. As shown throughout this analysis, youth participation is up in most cases, but involvement among older people is up even more, resulting in ever more generational inequality in political action. As Andrea Campbell concludes in her study of the rise of political activism among American senior citizens, "the crucial feature of mass politics in the United States is not the decline in participation, but the participatory divergence of young and old."[106] Thus, young people's participation in the forest of American political participation is being eclipsed by ever larger inputs from their elders. One can only hope that politicians will not ignore the smaller growing trees, as in the long run the future lies with them.

CHAPTER 8

Was Voting for Young People in the Obama Era?

"That's a scary statistic," said the director of LiveKC, an organization that seeks to make Kansas City an attractive place for Millennials, when he found out that in the April 2014 city election more people over the age of 90 voted than those under the age of 30.

> Source: Lynn Horsley, "Paltry Youth Voter Turnout in KC Raises Concerns," *Kansas City Star*, May 3, 2015 (http://www.kansascity.com/news/government-politics/article20151270.html, accessed October 1, 2015)

It has become almost conventional wisdom that Barack Obama's 2008 campaign owed its success in large part to the mobilization of the volunteer spirit of America's youth. Many observers have painted a legendary image of the Obama campaign plugging into the heretofore untapped power of the Internet to mobilize legions of young volunteers and spur record numbers of young Americans to vote. *Time* magazine even labeled 2008 as the "Year of the Youth Vote," noting that Obama was "tapping into a broad audience of energized young voters hungry for change."[107] The enthusiasm that so many young people displayed at massive rallies for Obama during the 2008 campaign led many observers to proclaim that the stereotype of politically apathetic American youth no longer rang true. For example, an article in *Wiretap* magazine proclaimed, "This year, the epithet of youth apathy was finally laid to rest." This article further observed, "The vast majority of pundits and mainstream media outlets recognized the power of the youth vote, thanks in part to the unprecedented volunteering among first-time voters."[108]

If such claims were accurate, many of the preceding chapters of this book would be obsolete, much like books about the Soviet Union proved to be after the sudden collapse of communism. However, a close examination of the data from the 2008 to 2014 elections reveals that claims about the end of the era of youth political apathy were way off the mark. Although there were some positive developments for young Americans' political involvement in 2008, young people were still clearly the least politically attentive age group, as well as the least likely to vote. Furthermore, once the stimulus of the initial Obama campaign had worn off, their political involvement returned to abysmal levels in subsequent elections, reaching rock bottom in 2014.

By declaring a premature end to the era of young people's political apathy, many observers were in effect taking Senator George Aiken's famous advice during the height of the Vietnam War—declare victory and go home. Of course, Senator Aiken did not really believe that victory could be achieved in Vietnam; his suggestion was merely a way of saying we had accomplished all we could in Vietnam and hence should give up trying any further. Political commentators who declared victory against youth apathy were essentially doing the same thing without realizing it. By declaring that the problem had been solved, they effectively took the pressure off politicians to do something about this sad state of affairs. This chapter will briefly review some of the major evidence from the 2008–2014 period that is relevant to this point.

Has the Internet Changed Age Patterns of Political Attention?

The 2008 presidential campaign was the first in which the Internet played a major role. In particular, the Obama campaign used the Internet to communicate with its supporters more widely and frequently than ever before. Because young people took to the Internet at the fastest rate, it is reasonable to hypothesize that age patterns of political attention may have undergone major changes from those reported earlier in this book. Hence, a reexamination of age patterns of political news consumption is in order. High levels of Internet usage to follow politics may now compensate for young people's relative lack of use of traditional media sources.

Just before the 2008 election, the Pew Research Center released a highly publicized report that revealed a huge growth in Internet usage in the campaign compared with 2004.[109] The crux of this report was that the Internet was now second only to television as a source of political information. Yet, with usage of the Internet now becoming mainstream, the edge that young people once enjoyed as early adopters of the medium had dissipated by 2008. As can be seen in Table 8.1, frequent Internet use to follow the 2008 campaign was just slightly higher among the two youngest age groups. Aside from the fact that senior citizens had still not taken to the Internet as a way of following politics, the age differences were unremarkable. And by 2012 the age differences had further leveled out, with middle-aged people being the heaviest consumers of campaign news on the Internet.

TABLE 8.1
Media Use to Follow Campaigns by Age Group

	18–29	30–44	45–64	65+
Read, watched, or listened to information on the Internet a good many times				
2012	14	18	17	14
2008	20	22	15	9
Watched a good many programs on TV				
2012	14	17	26	41
2008	21	33	40	51
Read a good many newspaper articles				
2012	6	9	14	28
2008	9	13	20	30
Listened to a good many radio programs				
2012	4	10	12	12
2008	13	19	23	18
Used at least one medium frequently				
2012	24	31	42	53
2008	40	52	59	63
Average # of frequent responses				
2012	.37	.53	.68	.97
2008	.62	.86	.97	1.07
Use of social media at least 5 days a week to learn about the 2012 campaign	37	22	15	10

Source: 2008 and 2012 American National Election Studies.

Similar results were reported by Matthew Hindman in his path-breaking book about the Internet and politics entitled *The Myth of Digital Democracy*.[110] Hindman acquired data from Hitwise.com, which tracked actual Internet clicks to a million individual websites from a sample of more than

10 million Internet subscribers. He found that the age profile of visitors to political sites, news sites, and political blogs virtually matched that of the adult population. As Hindman concluded, "While general Internet use overrepresents younger citizens, online politics does not."[111] In short, Internet clicking by young people has not made up for their continued underrepresentation among regular consumers of traditional news sources, such as newspapers and television.

The age pattern of frequent use of newspapers in the Obama elections shown in Table 8.1 is surely no surprise given the data from previous years reviewed in Chapter 1 of this book. What makes this picture even more striking now is the fiscal danger facing the newspaper business due to its inability to attract young readers. The Newspaper Association of America reported that the total circulation of newspapers in the United States declined by 26 percent between 2004 and 2014. Hopes that the Internet could be the financial savior for newspapers have been dashed, as Internet revenues have fallen far short of what is needed to maintain a full staff of newspaper reporters and editors. As of 2014, income received from digital channels represented only about 12 percent of newspaper revenues.[112]

With newspapers declining and the usage of the Internet still relatively limited when it comes to politics, television is likely to continue to be the dominant means of political communication in America for a while longer. Nevertheless, consumption of television programs to follow campaigns is clearly slipping. Between 2008 and 2012, the percentage of Americans who watched a good many programs on TV fell markedly among all age groups. As young people were the most likely to stop watching television, the audience for politics on TV is now older than ever before.

The propensity of older citizens to use TV to follow recent campaigns matches nicely with Nielsen data regarding who tunes in to the big networks these days. In Fall 2014, headlines blared that TV is increasingly for old people based on a study of Nielsen data which found that the median audience for the major networks had risen to 53.9.[113] Six years earlier, Steve Sternberg's "Median Age Report" told much the same story in greater detail, providing data on many specific shows and channels.[114] Sternberg found that each of the nightly network newscasts attracted an audience with a median age of 61. And the news magazine 60 Minutes could well derive its name from the average age of its audience. Of course, today's viewers also have alternatives to the 30-minute network news shows in the form of round-the-clock news on CNN, MSNBC, and the Fox News Channel. Cable news may well be different in terms of content and format than the traditional network news, but Sternberg found that the age distribution of its audience is virtually the same.

Having not developed the habit of watching the news when they were growing up in an era of multiple entertainment options, young viewers have bypassed news programs for shows like The Simpsons and Gossip Girl. And rather than tuning in to cable news, the Nielsen data reveal that young people clearly prefer to watch channels like Nike-at-Nite, MTV, VH1, Comedy, and E!.

Markus Prior's path-breaking work on post-broadcast democracy introduces the important concept of "Relative Entertainment Preference," which is basically the ratio of entertainment to news consumption on TV. Prior's careful analysis found that the only sizable predictor of this measure was age, with young people preferring entertainment by a wide margin, whereas older people leaned much more toward news and public affairs shows.[115] As Prior writes, "Unlike most other forms of inequality, however, this one arises due to voluntary consumption decisions. Entertainment fans abandon politics not because it has become harder for them to be involved ... but because they decide to devote their time to media that promise greater gratification than the news."[116] The result, he argues, is that those individuals with a preference for entertainment over news miss out on the "fanfare of a presidential campaign amid the hubbub of movie channels and reality contests."[117]

Taking all the data about following campaigns via TV, newspaper, radio, and the Internet together, we can now explore how many people within each age category said they had followed a campaign a lot through at least one medium. In both 2008 and 2012 the audience for campaign news was skewed toward older people, but this pattern was more apparent in 2012. Over half of senior citizens in 2012 reported that they had used at least one medium frequently to follow the campaign as compared to just 24 percent of respondents under the age of 30. Furthermore, senior citizens were also far more likely to report using multiple mediums frequently, with the result being that the mean number of mediums used by seniors to follow the 2012 campaign was .97 as compared to just .37 among young people.

Many students look at these patterns and ask: "What about social media?" After all, social media has reshaped American life in many ways recently. For the first time in 2012, the American National Election Study asked people how often in a typical week they had used social media to learn about the presidential election. As expected, young people made far more use of social media to learn about the campaign than other age groups. Whether or not social media can serve as a substitute for following campaigns through TV, newspaper, radio, and the Internet is an open question. At present, the correlation between following the campaign through social media and mass media is much greater for younger people than older people. Thirty percent of young respondents who frequently used social media to learn about the campaign also regularly used some traditional media form as compared to just 20 percent for those who weren't using social media to follow the campaign. This pattern would indicate that social media is more of a supplement for some young people's campaign exposure than a mode for replacing traditional media.

DID THE CAMPAIGNS REALLY REACH OUT TO YOUNG PEOPLE IN THE OBAMA ELECTIONS?

If young people didn't come to the campaign, perhaps the campaign came to them. An integral part of the Obama campaign's reputed ability to mobilize America's youth was its stated goal of contacting potential young voters in order to expand the size and scope of the electorate. Certainly, this can be seen as a noble goal designed to give young people their fair share of political attention after many years of relative neglect by campaigns and officeholders alike. Yet, the reality of the situation leads me to suspect that such claims about the Obama campaigns contacting young people in 2008 and 2012 probably had more bark than bite.

A perfectly rational strategy for any campaign is to focus its contacting resources on people who are 1) the most likely to vote and 2) the easiest to reach. To violate either of these principles would amount to an inefficient use of campaign resources. And, unfortunately, young people are the least likely to meet these criteria for efficient campaign contacts.

First, when a campaign invests resources to knock on a door, it ought to have a reasonable expectation that someone in the household will actually vote. The availability of computerized registration lists that detail each individual's recent history of voting has become an invaluable source of information for campaigns, making it easier than ever to target likely voters. A clear bias that results from such targeting is that young people who lack a track record of voting participation are less likely to meet this criterion for campaign contacts. Second, although phone banks enable campaigns to reach out to more individuals than is possible in person, young people are less likely to be on the receiving end simply because they are less likely to answer. Young people are more likely to be out at night when phone banks usually operate. Furthermore, the recent trend toward total reliance on cell phones among young adults has made them even more difficult for campaigns to reach via a phone call.[118] Most people are unlikely to answer a call from an unknown number on their cell phone. In addition, robo-dialing to cell phones is currently forbidden by federal communications law. Thus, young people who rely exclusively on cell phones will never be on the receiving end of the pre-recorded political messages that many campaigns employ today. In sum, there is good reason to expect that campaign contacts have increasingly slighted young people in recent years, notwithstanding the Obama campaign's stated goal of incorporating youth.

The available data from the quadrennial American National Election Studies are ideal for testing whether the pattern of campaign contacts by age has indeed changed over time. Since 1956, these surveys have asked the following question in each presidential election: "As you know, the political parties try to talk to as many people as they can to get them to vote for their candidate. Did anyone from one of the political parties call you up or come around and talk to you about the campaign this year?" The percentage of people who reported some sort of contact is

displayed for each age group in Figure 8.1. Notably, between 1956
and 1972, personal and phone contacts by the campaigns were
fairly evenly distributed over all four age categories. Then from
1976 to 1992, contacts with young people steadily declined while
holding fairly steady among the oldest two groups. Since 1996,
campaign contacts have grown at an amazing rate, with the parties
focusing increasingly on mobilizing the elderly as opposed to
young people. This trend continued unabated in the Obama elections. In the Obama–McCain contest, 65 percent of senior citizens
reported that they had been contacted by a campaign as compared
to a mere 25 percent among respondents under 30 years of age.
In the Obama–Romney contest, contacts with young people fell to
just 14 percent – nearly the lowest ever – whereas contacts with the
elderly held at the all-time high of 65 percent.

As startling as these data are, this simple measure actually
underestimates how much the campaigns now concentrate their

FIGURE 8.1
Party Contacting During Election Campaigns by Age, 1956–2012

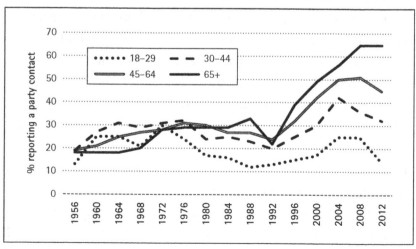

Source: 1956–2012, American National Elections Studies.

mobilization efforts on the elderly. A follow-up question probes those who have been contacted as to which party, or parties, contacted them. The elderly are such a prime catch for the parties that the percentage who reported that *both* Democrats and Republicans contacted them was 30 percent in 2008 and 31 percent in 2012, as compared to a mere 4 percent among young people in 2008 and 3 percent in 2012. All told, for every 100 senior citizens, the campaigns made 94 voter contacts during the Obama elections; by contrast, for every 100 young people, the parties made just 23 contacts.

One possible criticism of this measure of voter contacts is that it does not take into account electronic contacts from the campaigns. In particular, with young people being so reliant on e-mail, text messages, Twitter, and Facebook, it may be that they were reached in great numbers this way. Fortunately, the Pew Research Center's 2008 and 2012 post-election surveys asked some questions about electronic contacts from the campaigns. In 2008, only 24 percent of people under 30 reported receiving an e-mail from a campaign. Middle-aged citizens were slightly more likely to report e-mail contact (28 percent), with only the elderly trailing in this respect (15 percent). Reflecting the expansion of electronic means of communication by 2012, the Pew Center asked two questions this time—one on campaign contacts via e-mail or text message, and another on contacts via Facebook, Twitter, or some other social network. Combining the results of the two questions reveals that 29 percent of young respondents received some form of electronic communication from a presidential campaign in 2012. As in 2008, the figures for other age groups reveal slightly more contacts among middle-aged citizens (34 percent) and slightly fewer among the elderly (24 percent). In sum, these results show little evidence that electronic contacts from the campaigns to young people make up for their lack of traditional face-to-face and telephone contact. Even with the new forms of electronic communication available to them, the campaigns are still short-changing young people in their mobilization efforts.

Given that young people did not follow politics closely through the mass media in the Obama elections and the campaign organizations did not contact many of them, there is reason to doubt whether the Obama elections substantially reversed the trends in youth election participation. The next two sections will review the data on two key questions in this regard. First, did young people really turn out in unprecedented numbers to propel Obama toward the Democratic nomination in 2008, as is often claimed? And, second, did young people participate in higher numbers in the general elections of 2008 and 2012?

How Much Did Young People Participate in the 2008 Nomination Process?

From the beginning of the 2008 nomination process on a cold January night in Iowa through to the last primaries, many stories circulated regarding the seemingly high rates of participation of young people. In particular, the much-reported contribution of young people to Obama's crucial breakthrough in Iowa set the tone for the coverage of young people in the 2008 campaign. The Iowa exit polls estimated that 22 percent of the 240,000 Democrats who attended the caucuses were under the age of 30, as were 11 percent of the 122,000 participants on the Republican side. All told, this amounted to approximately 65,000 young Iowans showing up at 7 p.m. at a specific place to make their presidential preferences heard.

Why so many observers interpreted these numbers as indicating a newsworthy surge in youth participation is difficult to fathom. According to the Census Bureau, the size of the 18- to 29-year-old age group in Iowa was about 501,000 in 2008. Thus, the involvement of 65,000 young people represented a turnout rate of just 13 percent. Granted, given the substantial time commitment that caucus attendance requires, this percentage might seem to be pretty good. But in Iowa, what with the massive media attention devoted to the nation's first test of the presidential candidates, the overall turnout rate was 16 percent of the voting-age population. It is hard to see why a below-average rate of participation among young people was seemingly so newsworthy.

Furthermore, there is good reason to believe that the 2008 Iowa exit poll may have overestimated the participation of young voters. Exit polls are employed by the media in order to provide them with a rough sense of how various groups have voted; they are not designed to provide an accurate measurement of group turnout rates. Michael McDonald has carefully compared estimates of group turnout rates from exit polls to the actual computerized records from some states. He finds that exit polls consistently report that young people make up a significantly larger percentage of voters than official records indicate was actually the case, and vice versa for the elderly. McDonald wisely counsels consumers of exit polls "to await confirming evidence before reaching conclusions about the age and race composition of the electorate."[119]

Although McDonald's evidence comes from a general election, his point certainly applies to primary voting as well. For example, the data from exit polls conducted for the 2008 Georgia presidential primary produce an estimated turnout of 18 percent for people under 30, compared to 26 percent among senior citizens. However, months later Georgia's Secretary of State published a report based on the records of who cast ballots which revealed that the turnout differences between these groups were actually much greater— just 12 percent of young people voted, compared to 40 percent of the elderly.[120]

Table 8.2 displays the official 2008 data regarding the turnout within each age category in Georgia, as well as three other states for which such voter records from the primaries are readily available. While these four states can hardly be considered to be representative of the 40 states that held primaries, the relationship

TABLE 8.2
Turnout by Age in the 2008 Presidential Primaries

	18–24	25–34	35–44	45–54	55–64	65+	OLDEST/YOUNGEST RATIO
GA	10	18	27	34	41	40	4.0 : 1

	18–24	25–34	35–49		50–61	62+	OLDEST/YOUNGEST RATIO
KY	12	18	26		36	40	3.3 : 1

	18–21	22–44			45–64	65+	OLDEST/YOUNGEST RATIO
SC	10	20			36	40	4.0 : 1

	18–34	35–49			50–64	65+	OLDEST/YOUNGEST RATIO
CA*	20	37			54	62	3.1 : 1

*Because of the very high percentage of non-citizens in California, these data are adjusted to exclude non-citizens based on Census Bureau survey data. (Such adjustments would make much less difference in the other states, which have smaller proportions of non-citizens. Furthermore, the size of the Census sample for the other states is insufficient to provide reliable estimates of non-citizens within each age category.)

Sources: Actual numbers of voters within each age group were provided by Georgia Secretary of State; Kentucky State Board of Elections; South Carolina State Election Commission; and Datamar (http://www.datamar.net/pdf/cappvoterturnout2008.pdf). Population estimates within each age group are from the U.S. Census Bureau.

between age and turnout in each is remarkably consistent. Participation rates increased substantially from ages 18 to about 60, and then leveled off at a plateau that was three to four times higher than found for the youngest age group. Once again, as stated in Chapter 4, a huge percentage of young people acted as if primary elections were parties they were not invited to. Imagine the outrage that would occur if the political parties passed resolutions giving each senior citizen the chance to cast three votes in primary contests while limiting young people to just one vote. The practical impact of the 2008 turnout patterns in these states effectively gave senior citizens just such an advantage over young people.

Yet, rather than recognizing the generational inequities in these participation rates, the media focused instead on the crucial role that young people played in Obama's nomination victory. Given that exit polls routinely showed that young Democratic voters preferred Obama over Hillary Clinton by at least a 60–40 margin, it would be hard to deny that they provided his campaign with an important edge. Given the closeness of the battle between Obama and Clinton for the nomination, even a 60–40 split within a group with a low turnout rate clearly mattered. Yet, consider how much different the contest would have been had young people's turnout rate in the primaries been equal to that of senior citizens (who clearly favored Clinton over Obama). An exceedingly small national margin for Obama would have been transformed into a reasonably definitive Obama victory.

If one wants to identify a group that really provided a major boost for Obama in the primaries, it makes far more sense to look to African-Americans. In most states, Blacks supported Obama over Clinton by at least a four-to-one margin, and reliable data point to a clear mobilization on their part. Democratic primary turnout was up across the board due to the unusual level of public interest in the Obama–Clinton contest. But the fact that the percentage of Democratic primary voters who were Black increased dramatically between 2004 and 2008 indicates that the African-American turnout went up disproportionately. Official statistics from Louisiana and Georgia—two states that are still required to keep track of the race of their voters due to the Voting Rights Act—effectively illustrates this point. In Louisiana, the percentage of Democratic primary voters who were African-American increased from 42 percent in 2004 to 57 percent in 2008. The figures in Georgia were nearly identical, as the African-American proportion increased from 41 to 58 percent.

It would be hard to argue that the Black mobilization in the 2008 primaries was a youth phenomenon based on the data from Georgia, which is the only state to have released statistics by racial/age combinations. Only 19 percent of registered Blacks under the age of 25 cast votes in the Democratic primary, as compared to 59 percent among registered Black senior citizens.[121] In short, even among an ethnic minority that saw its participation rate increase substantially, the primary turnout was heavily skewed toward the elderly.

PARTICIPATION RATES BY AGE IN THE 2008 AND 2012 GENERAL ELECTIONS

It is more plausible to hypothesize that young minorities were particularly mobilized in the 2008 general election, when interest in the Obama candidacy peaked, than in the primaries. As Chapter 4 showed, turnout differences by age are always at their lowest in the final act of presidential contests. Because the elderly already have such high general election turnout rates, any mobilization effects are especially likely to be found among the young.

Given that turnout increases in 2008 were concentrated in states with large minority populations, if there is any validity to the notion of "the year of the youth vote," it seems most likely to be found among young minority group members.

The Census Bureau's biennial survey of voting participation provides an ideal source of data to test this hypothesis regarding turnout rates of young minorities. With a national sample size of about 100,000 individuals of voting age, it is possible to estimate turnout rates among even relatively small groups within the population. Table 8.3 displays the reported turnouts of Blacks, Hispanics, Asians, and non-Hispanic White citizens by age category between 2004 and 2012. The data clearly support the supposition that voter mobilization in 2008 occurred predominately among young racial minorities. In particular, the survey found that the turnout among Blacks under the age of 30 rose from 49 percent in 2004 to 58 percent in the Obama–McCain contest. By contrast, the turnout rate of Black senior citizens rose by only 2 percent.

It is notable that the excitement of having the nation's first racial minority nominated for president extended beyond the African-American community. Young Hispanic and Asian citizens also saw their turnout rates increase markedly between 2004 and 2008. The increase in voting participation among Hispanics and Asians was particularly concentrated among young people; unlike Black senior citizens, the turnout rates of Hispanics and Asians over the age of 65 actually declined slightly in 2008.

Although the substantial increase in young minority turnout was certainly good news, it was unfortunately tempered by the stagnant turnout figures of young non-Hispanic Whites. In both 2004 and 2008, the reported turnout rate of this group—which represents two-thirds of all American citizens under the age of

TABLE 8.3
Turnout by Age and Race in the General Elections of 2004 to 2012

	18–29	30–44	45–64	65+
2004 White, non hispanic	52.3	65.6	73.2	73.1
2008 White, non hispanic	52.1	64.2	71.2	72.6
2012 White, non hispanic	46.1	61.2	69.5	73.4
Change 2004–08	*−0.2*	*−1.4*	*−2.0*	*−0.5*
Change 2008–12	*−6.0*	*−3.0*	*−1.7*	*+0.8*
2004 Black	49.1	61.3	65.3	65.8
2008 Black	58.0	65.0	68.7	67.7
2012 Black	53.4	66.1	72.4	74.6
Change 2004–08	*+8.9*	*+3.7*	*+3.4*	*+1.9*
Change 2008–12	*−4.6*	*+1.1*	*+3.7*	*+6.9*
2004 Hispanic	35.4	47.4	56.2	57.0
2008 Hispanic	40.7	49.3	58.1	56.0
2012 Hispanic	36.9	48.6	55.6	59.9
Change 2004–08	*+5.3*	*+1.9*	*+1.9*	*−1.0*
Change 2008–12	*−3.8*	*−0.7*	*−2.5*	*+3.3*
2004 Asian	34.1	45.0	52.4	48.0
2008 Asian	42.8	49.4	51.3	44.9
2012 Asian	38.0	48.1	51.8	54.1
Change 2004–08	*+8.7*	*+4.4*	*−1.1*	*−3.1*
Change 2008–12	*−4.8*	*−1.3*	*+0.5*	*+9.2*

Source: 2004–2012 U.S. Census Bureau Voting and Registration Surveys (non-citizens excluded).

30—was just 52 percent. Because the turnout did not rise among this segment of young people, the overall increase for 18-to-29-year-olds was limited to just 2 percent.

One possible reason for optimism about young people's turnout rates following the 2008 election was that many scholars believe that voting is a habit. The increase in turnout among young minorities was quite reasonably seen by some observers as the first step toward making voting a more regular behavior for them. And with the chance to reelect Obama in 2012, there was definitely a chance that the enthusiasm of 2008 could be rekindled. Indeed, Mitt Romney, as well as other prominent Republicans, reflected after the 2012 election that they were stunned at the size of the minority turnout, which of course benefited President Obama. Thus, one might reasonably hypothesize that the 2012 Obama campaign was able to further mobilize young minorities to vote.

However, returning to Table 8.3, the 2012 Census Bureau data by race and age tell a much less sanguine story. Among young citizens under the age of 30, all three minority groups saw substantial declines in turnout betweeen the first and second Obama elections. In contrast, among minority senior citizens (those over age 65) there was a notable turnout increase, especially for Blacks and Asians. The net result was that the age pattern for the turnout of minority groups in 2012 looked pretty similar to that found for non-Hispanic Whites. Thus, the problem of young people being severely underrepresented at the polls was once again clearly in evidence in 2012.

Finally, we can explore other forms of participation in the 2008 and 2012 elections via the American National Election Studies for these years. Table 8.4 presents data on four separate questions which these surveys posed in both Obama victories. In 2008, there was little relationship between age and active forms of participation in the campaign (e.g., those beyond simply voting). Senior citizens were roughly as likely to go to a political meeting, display a political campaign item, or do some work for a party or candidate as were middle-aged and younger people. The only aspect in which senior citizens participated at above-average rates in 2008 was in giving campaign money—a pattern that naturally stems from their greater financial resources.

TABLE 8.4

Campaign Participation in 2008 and 2012 by Age

	18–29	30–44	45–64	65+
Go to a political meeting/rally/speech/dinner				
2008	9	7	11	5
2012	3	3	5	15
Change	–6	–4	–6	+10
Display button/sticker/sign				
2008	18	16	21	15
2012	11	9	13	21
Change	–7	–7	–8	+6
Other work for party/candidate				
2008	4	4	5	3
2012	1	2	3	7
Change	–3	–2	–2	+4
Contribute $ to campaign/party/group supporting candidate				
2008	10	11	20	18
2012	2	11	14	23
Change	–8	0	–6	+5
Some form of active campaign participation				
2008	24	22	31	23
2012	15	17	20	32
Change	–9	–5	–11	+9

Source: 2008 and 2012, American National Election Studies.

In contrast, in 2012 senior citizens were the most likely to take part in *all* active forms of campaign participation. As with turnout, senior citizens were the only group to take an even more active role in the 2012 campaign than in 2008. The last segment of Table 8.4 summarizes the picture of campaign activity, measuring whether a respondent had taken part in any of the four areas of campaign activity the ANES asked about beyond voting. Between 2008 and 2012, the percentage of senior citizens who were active participants in the campaign increased from 23 to 32 percent, whereas among young people campaign involvement declined from 24 to 15 percent.

In sum, just as it is often argued in the literature on economic equality that the rich are becoming richer, so it is that senior citizens are extending their advantage over young people in terms of electoral participation. Nowhere is this pattern more evident than in midterm elections, to which we turn next.

Where Did All the Young Voters Go in the 2010 and 2014 Midterms?

As the 2010 campaign came to a close, President Obama and his advisers realized that young people's apparent lack of enthusiasm for voting in the midterm elections posed a substantial problem for them. Hence, the president went out of his way to make a number of high-profile speeches before young audiences, such as at the University of Wisconsin and the University of Maryland. Obama also took part in a youth town hall event televised on MTV and granted an unprecedented 22-minute interview to comedian Jon Stewart for Comedy Central's *The Daily Show*. The president's message to young people was that if they cared about the change agenda of 2008, then they couldn't sit out the 2010 contest. As he told a group of college journalists in September 2010, "Democracy is never a one and done proposition. It is something that requires sustained engagement and sustained involvement."[122]

Sustained political involvement, however, requires sustained attention to unfolding events in the political world. But as seen earlier in this chapter, even amidst the excitement of the 2008 campaign young Americans were not regular consumers of political information. Being generally less attentive to politics was evident in young people's relatively low interest in, and knowledge of, Congress in 2008. Only 16 percent of young respondents to the ANES said that they cared very much about how the House contests came out in 2008, compared to 45 percent of seniors; similarly, just 24 percent of the former knew that the Democrats had the most members in the House prior to the election, compared to 52 percent of the latter. If young people were so relatively inattentive to congressional politics in 2008, then they were scarcely likely to vote without the stimulus of a presidential campaign. Indeed, this was just what happened in both midterm elections of the Obama era.

According to the Census Bureau's surveys of voter turnout, the participation of citizens under the age of 30 dropped precipitously from 51 percent in 2008 to just 24 percent in 2010. By contrast, senior citizens saw their turnout rate fall much less, from 70 percent in 2008 to a still-impressive 61 percent in 2010. These disparate patterns led young adults to be sadly underrepresented at the polls during this midterm election. Although young people constituted 22 percent of all adult citizens, they cast only 10 percent of the ballots in 2010.

In 2014, turnout fell across the nation to its lowest level in over 70 years, with just 36 percent of citizens participating in the crucial elections that yielded Republican majorities in both chambers of

Congress for the first time in the Obama era. The Census Bureau's national survey revealed that just 20 percent of citizens under the age of 30 voted, the lowest such figure ever recorded. Even worse, their registration rate also fell to a new low, indicating a woeful level of political interest.

Figure 8.2 displays the drop-off in turnout by age in Iowa, a state that has consistently had relatively high electoral participation. Iowa's battleground status led it to have the 4th highest turnout rate in the nation in 2012, and in 2014 it ranked 7th due to its highly competitive Senate race. Among senior citizens in Iowa, the interest generated by these elections yielded laudable turnout rates of 79 percent in 2012 and 71 percent in 2014. If the entire nation could have turnout rates like this, we could probably rest satisfied that America's turnout problem had been solved. But, as Figure 8.2

FIGURE 8.2
Turnout Drop-off in Iowa by Age Group, 2012–2014

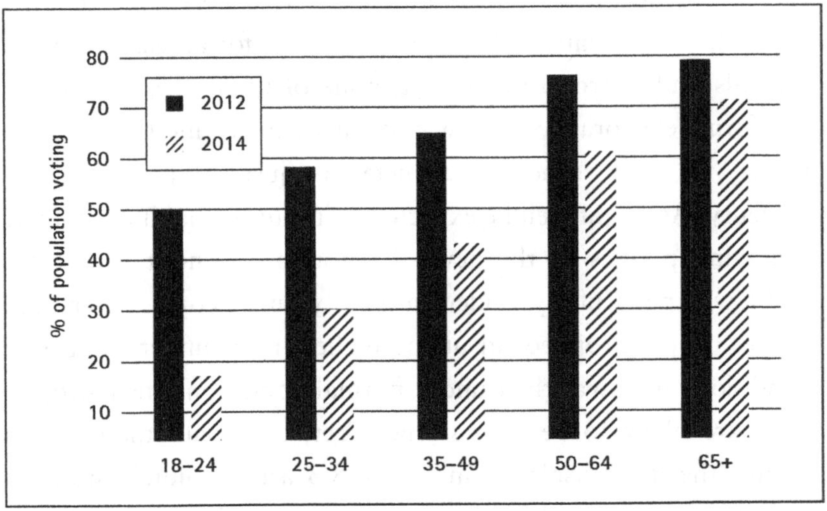

Source: Actual numbers of voters within each age group were provided by the Iowa Secretary of State. Population estimates within each age group are from the U.S. Census Bureau.

graphically displays, the younger the group the more turnout dropped off during the midterm election. Senior citizens in Iowa were
more than 4 times more likely to vote in 2014 than those aged 18
to 24!

While Iowa provided exceptional stimulus to vote in both
years, many other states experienced little such political competition to motivate turnout. It is thus crucial to examine how different
age groups fared under more normal circumstances, as most states
are not battlegrounds in presidential elections, nor lucky enough to
have a hotly contested statewide election in a midterm. California,
home to about one-eighth of the nation's population provides an
excellent example.

With California all but certain to go for Obama, the
presidential candidates ran no ads in the state's media markets in
2012 and stopped by only to raise money and tape appearances on
national TV shows like the "Tonight Show." Nevertheless, 55
percent of California's citizens voted, spurred no doubt by the
excitement of a fairly close national presidential race. Two years
later, all Californians had the chance to vote for at least 12 elected
officials and 6 propositions. Yet, none of these races excited the
California electorate, with few close races all around the state. The
result was that turnout plummeted to just 30 percent of the
citizenry. As might well be expected, without the habit of regularly
following politics in the news, California's turnout drop-off in
2014 was particularly evident among young people. After all, if
young people dropped off at the highest rates under the best of
conditions in Iowa, then under normal conditions their drop-off
rates are likely to be even steeper. Yet, even with these expectations, the data displayed in Figure 8.3 are absolutely stunning.
Just 8 percent of California citizens between the ages of 18 and
24 cast a ballot in 2014 according to an analysis of the actual voter

files analyzed by the California Civic Engagement Project at UC, Davis.[123] Being more regular news consumers, older people showed much higher levels of turnout. Californians between the ages of 65 and 74 were seven times more likely to cast a ballot than 18-to-24-year-olds, and even people over the age of 75 were more than six times as likely to vote as California's young citizens.

Lest one think that California is an aberrant example, data from New York City provide another amazing case of low youth turnout. The city's Voter Assistance Advisory Committee found that just 11 percent of registered voters between the ages of 18 and 29 voted. Adjusting for the typical 60 percent registration rate amongst this age group, this would mean that about 7 percent of young citizens living in the Big Apple voted in 2014. As the

FIGURE 8.3

Turnout Drop-off in California by Age Group, 2012–2014

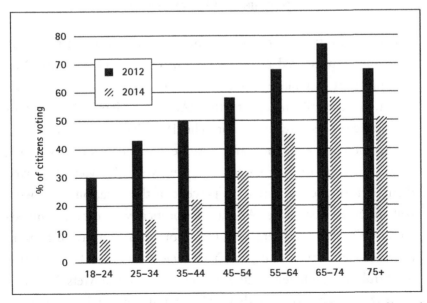

Source: California Civic Engagement Project, UC, Davis based on California voter files and U.S. Census Bureau estimates of citizens within each age category.

New York Daily News put it in its inimitable way, this report was "a reminder that voter turnout stinks."[124]

In short, most young people passed up their chance to vote in the 2010 and 2014 midterm elections that gave huge gains to the Republicans, thereby setting up a roadblock for Obama's agenda. The fact that young people, who have consistently been among the most supportive groups for President Obama, had such a low turnout rate in the midterm elections was highly damaging to Democratic prospects at the polls. My rough estimate is that had turnout rates been equal among all age groups, the Democratic percentage of the congressional vote would have been about 1.7 percent higher— clearly enough to enable the Democrats to hold on to substantially more seats. Who votes does make a difference.

CONCLUSION: LAST PLACE IN TURNOUT IS NOTHING TO CROW ABOUT

It is certainly true that young people's involvement in the 2008 campaign represented an improvement over previous years. Yet, coming in at last place in election turnout was nothing to crow about. A baseball analogy to the "Amazing Mets" of the 1960s should help illustrate this point. The 1962 New York Mets were the worst team ever in Major League Baseball history, winning only 25 percent of their games. The next year, the Mets improved their performance, winning 32 percent of the time, but they were still mired in last place. At least theoretically, sports columnists could write that the Mets were the second most improved team in the National League that year. Yet, given their woeful record, it is doubtful anyone labeled 1963 as the "Year of the Mets." Calling 2008 the "Year of the Youth Vote" is equally far-fetched in light of the dismal turnout statistics for young people. Young people's turnout rates hit a low for presidential elections in 1996; each of the next three presidential elections saw some improvement. Yet, as shown in this chapter, young people were still in last place in the turnout competition throughout the Obama era. Since when is a regular last-place finish something to crow about?

An optimist might note that the lowly Mets of the early 1960s were amazingly transformed into the World Champions of baseball by 1969. Some observers apparently thought that young people's involvement in politics was on just such a positive trajectory in 2008. However, unlike the early Mets, there is no reason to expect that young people will soon have the resources to pull themselves out of last place in terms of election turnout. Early on in their history, the Mets established a loyal fan base that brought a good deal of money into the team, which was then invested in young players. Furthermore, the institution of the Major League draft in 1965 gave struggling teams like the Mets first crack at the best players. These resources were key in turning the team's fortunes around quickly. As this chapter has shown, young Americans in the age of Obama continued to lack the resources that could boost their electoral participation rates, namely a regular interest in following politics. As a result, their turnout rates remained mired in last place, and by 2014 they had fallen to below 10 percent in some parts of the country.

As long as young people continue to have such relatively little interest in political news and public affairs, it is hard to see how their turnout rates will catch up to those of their elders unless something is done. The good news is that something *can* be done if our political leaders have the will and the wisdom to do so. The next chapter reviews some of the potential courses of action.

CHAPTER 9

What Can Be Done?

In Australia, and some other countries, there's mandatory voting. It would be transformative if everybody voted. ... If everybody voted, then it would completely change the political map in this country, because the people who tend not to vote are young.

President Barack Obama, March 18, 2015

What can be done to ensure that voting is for young people just as much as it is for other age groups? There is no shortage of ideas among scholars and political commentators. All of these ideas are certainly well intentioned, and I have no qualms in recommending any of them. But if one really wants to solve the problem, and not just make a dent in it, then only one proven solution exists. In the end, I have to agree with Arend Lijphart, who has persuasively argued that "Compulsory voting is the only institutional mechanism ... that can assure high turnout virtually by itself."[125] This chapter explains how I arrived at this conclusion, first reviewing the other major proposals and then explaining why compulsory voting appears to be the only definitive answer to the problem.

How to Improve Turnout Rates
Without Compulsory Voting

When I discuss with my students the topic of low youth turnout, one of the most common suggestions they offer is that society should focus on improving civic education. No doubt this could only help boost turnout. As Niemi and Junn's careful research shows, a school civics curriculum enhances what students know about government and politics.[126] And, as this book has shown, the lack of political information among young adults is certainly a major source of the problem. In particular, students could benefit greatly from an educational program that teaches them why politics matters to all citizens, as well as to them personally. Even if everyone were suddenly to vote, we would still want to work on civic education in order to foster better-informed voters. The fact that so many young adults don't vote makes the imperative for increased civic education all the more vital.

Yet it must be kept in mind that a concerted effort to increase civic education will yield results only among those who are fairly receptive to being educated. It could thus accentuate the socio-economic bias at the polls that was Lijphart's primary concern when he addressed the problem of unequal political participation. Furthermore, any impact from improved civic education is bound to take a long time before becoming evident. The generations who have already left school without picking up the habit of following politics need to be brought into the political system as well, and even the best civic education programs are unlikely to reach many of these young adults.

Because most of my students are Americans, they naturally tend to mention aspects of U.S. campaigns that could be improved so as to facilitate citizen participation. One item that always comes up is making the process of voter registration easier. Because young Americans must register in order to cast their first ballot, and are then likely to be faced with reregistering due to their high levels of mobility, the barriers posed by American registration laws fall most heavily on them. Therefore, anything that can be done to make registration procedures more user-friendly should theoretically benefit young people more than other age groups. State laws that continue to require citizens to register 30 days prior to an election now seem like a product of 20th-century record-keeping technology. With 21st-century computer technology making it possible to update registration files far more expeditiously than in the past, everyone should be given the maximum opportunity to register to vote.

In 2015, Oregon took a huge step toward increasing registration rates by enacting the first automatic registration system in the country. Oregon's Department of Motor Vehicles will now transmit information about citizens to the Secretary of State's Office for the purpose of registering these people to vote or updating their registration. Individuals who are automatically registered or reregistered will be sent a notice stating their new voter registration details and will have the option to opt out of being registered if they so choose. In other words, this is a revolutionary change from one that puts the onus on the individual to opt in to one in which the individual has to take an action not to be registered. It is estimated that 300,000 more individuals will be registered in Oregon in 2016, bringing the registration rate in the state to 87 percent of its citizenry. No doubt this will boost the registration of young Oregonians more than that of any other age group.

Although it seems good sense to make registration as easy as possible without inviting fraud, even the best registration procedures are unlikely to solve the problem of low youth turnout.

Registration has been made significantly easier in the United States over the last four decades—most notably by the passage of the 1993 Motor Voter Act, which required states to permit people to register when they apply for or renew their driver's licenses. Nevertheless, just 54 percent of 18- to 24-year-old citizens were registered to vote in 2012 as compared to 61 percent in 1972.[127] The next major step in registration reform would be to provide for election day registration, or a comprehensive voter list compiled by the government. Canada permits election day registration throughout the whole country, but it has seen a substantial age gap in turnout develop nonetheless. The governments of Japan and Switzerland compile comprehensive voter registration lists that could serve as models for any country, but getting their young adults to vote has proved far more difficult than getting them registered in recent years.

If the problem of getting young people to vote stems mostly from a lack of exposure to politics, as this book argues, then it is no wonder that the results from registration reform have been disappointing. Removing barriers to voting will not have much of an effect if potential voters are not learning much about campaigns for office. Thomas Patterson focuses his attention in *The Vanishing Voter* on the obstacles to learning imposed by the poor design features of American campaigns.[128] Interestingly, Patterson argues that Americans are *over*exposed to presidential campaigns that seem to go on endlessly, concluding that "Nothing would breathe more life into the campaign than shortening it substantially."[129] However, an examination of the survey data collected for Patterson's project reveals that young adults were the least bothered by the length of the 2000 presidential campaign. Forty-nine percent of respondents under 30 said that they preferred a long campaign because it gave them a better chance to know the candidates, compared to 41 percent among respondents aged 30 to 64, and just 28 percent of senior citizens.[130] If one wants to see how shorter campaigns work in practice, one has only to turn to Britain and Canada. Both countries are noted for practicing short electoral campaigns on the order of four to six weeks; yet, their turnout rates have recently fallen to modern lows due to the poor participation rates of their young adults.

This is not to challenge Patterson's basic argument that American turnout rates could be marginally improved via a variety of good government reforms. A system of regional primaries would give the people of every state a meaningful role in choosing the major party candidates. Eliminating the electoral college would give the parties an incentive to mobilize voters in every state rather than focus on just the battleground states. And blocks of free TV time for the major parties on every channel could get information about the issues out to more voters.

My own favorite suggestion for improving American turnout involves a simple change in election timing. With an ordinary act of Congress, the date for federal elections could be moved to a leisure day, thereby giving more people more time during election day to vote. The number-one reason that people who are registered but fail to vote give for not participating is that they were too busy with work or school on election day. This excuse is particularly prevalent among young people.[131] So why not change election day from a Tuesday to a weekend or holiday? It is doubtful that any expert on elections would recommend that Afghanistan and Iraq emulate the American example of voting on a Tuesday; so if we wouldn't recommend Tuesday elections to other countries, why should we continue this practice ourselves? By joining the modern world and voting on a leisure day, it is likely that we would experience some increase in election turnout, especially among young people. Yet this suggestion also falls far short of being a panacea when viewed in comparative perspective. Countries that vote in the middle of the week, such as the United States, Canada, Britain, and Ireland, are experiencing low turnout among young people, but so are a number of other countries that vote on the weekend, such as New Zealand, Norway, Japan, and Switzerland.

Much the same case can be made for proportional representation, which has become part and parcel of a modern electoral system. Few experts today would suggest that a new democracy adopt a single-member district system such as long practiced in Britain, Canada, and the United States. Electoral systems that use some form of proportional representation ensure that votes for all the major parties end up counting, especially those for newer protest parties, which tend to draw support primarily from young people. However, New Zealand's experience as the first Anglo-American country to change to proportional representation would seem to indicate that such a switch has no more than a marginally positive impact on turnout.[132]

In sum, all of these proposals are worthy suggestions, but even combined they do not amount to a cure-all for generational disparities in turnout. This conclusion should hardly be surprising in light of the findings of Chapters 1–3 of this book, which demonstrated that recent generations have established modern lows for newspaper reading, TV news watching, and knowledge of public affairs. These new generational gaps in following politics are beyond the ability of any governmental reform to reverse. A government of a free country can hardly mandate that people pay attention to political news.

Want a Solution? Consider
Compulsory Voting

Some democracies do, however, require that adult citizens participate in elections or face a small fine.[133] This practice is commonly known as "compulsory voting," but it should be noted that this term is somewhat misleading. The secrecy of modern ballots makes it impossible to tell whether an individual has actually voted as opposed to just turned in a blank ballot. Thus, all that can really be required is that citizens show up for elections, not that they vote. But given that almost all people who go to the polls under this requirement do indeed make a choice of whom to vote for, and that "compulsory voting" is the commonly used phrase, it seems reasonable to use it here, with this caveat.

A compulsory voting law may seem strange to the American ear, but it is an idea that has been tried in a fair number of other countries. Of the 18 established democracies that have been covered in this book, Belgium and Australia have practiced compulsory voting throughout the post-World War II period. If one broadens the sphere a bit to all advanced industrialized societies, then Greece (a democracy since 1974) and tiny Luxembourg can also be added to the list of countries that presently require election attendance by law. In addition, Italy, Austria, and the Netherlands had compulsory voting laws on the books for at least part of the modern era, though enforcement in each of these countries was always weak. By comparison, among the same set of countries, only France, Finland, and the United States elect a president who plays a major role in governing. Thus, presidential government is actually rarer in wealthy democracies than is the practice of requiring citizens to go to the polls.

TABLE 9.1

Percent Reporting Casting a Ballot by Age in Advanced
Industrialized Countries that Currently Have or Recently
Had Compulsory Voting Laws

	<30	30–44	45–64	65+	OLDEST/YOUNGEST RATIO
Austria 2002*	82	90	92	90	1.1 : 1
Netherlands 1998*	88	91	92	94	1.1 : 1
Italy 2001*	89	92	93	86	1.0 : 1
Australia 2004**	97	98	98	99	1.0 : 1
Belgium 2004**	89	98	97	92	1.0 : 1
Greece 2000**	90	93	95	93	1.0 : 1
Luxembourg 1999**	91	93	95	86[v]	.9 : 1

* Recently had a compulsory voting law, but it is no longer in effect.
** Compulsory voting in effect.
[v]Voting is voluntary for citizens aged 70 and over in Luxembourg.
Note: Age is as of the election (not the survey) for Luxembourg, Greece, Italy, and Austria.
Sources: Netherlands, Australia, Belgium: Comparative Study of Electoral Systems; Luxembourg, Greece, Italy, Austria: 2002–2003 European Social Survey.

The best argument for the adoption of compulsory voting is simply that it works extremely well. As Arend Lijphart writes, "Compulsory voting is a particularly effective method to achieve high turnout," even with low penalties and lax enforcement.[134] In particular, the data displayed in Table 9.1 demonstrate that *compulsory voting laws get all age groups out to vote in very high numbers.* The relationship between age and turnout is negligible in all four advanced industrialized countries that currently practice compulsory voting. Unlike many other democracies that are suffering from abysmally low youth turnout, these four countries can boast turnout rates ranging from 89 to 97 percent among citizens aged 18 to 29.

Furthermore, the impact of compulsory voting laws seems to leave a participatory imprint on societies that continues to be felt even after the practice lapses. Austria, Italy, and the Netherlands no longer require their citizens to vote, but the fact that they formerly did has probably contributed to their continued very high participation rates. Even young people in these countries are voting at high rates, as shown in Table 9.1, perhaps because they have grown up in a country where the government made turnout a high priority at some point and required citizen participation.

How Much Support is There for Compulsory Voting?

One of the most common arguments against the adoption of compulsory voting is that the public just won't stand for it in countries where it is not already in place. How much truth is there in such an assertion? And how much support is there for compulsory voting in countries such as Australia, Belgium, Greece, and Luxembourg, where it is being successfully practiced at the present time? The answers are difficult to ascertain given that no cross-national survey has yet asked a question about compulsory voting. However, some country-specific data are available for Australia, Great Britain, Canada, and the United States, and these are displayed in Table 9.2.

The survey data from Australia demonstrate that compulsory voting has proved to be a widely popular policy there. Seventy-four percent of respondents to the 2004 Australian Election Study thought that voting at federal elections should be required, and of these people about two out of three said they strongly favored compulsory voting. Such high levels of support have consistently been the case in Australia, with support never falling below

TABLE 9.2
Support for Compulsory Voting in Australia, Canada, the UK, and the USA by Age (Percentage)

	18–29	30–44	45–64	65+	ALL
Support compulsory voting					
Australia	75	76	75	74	75
Great Britain	37	47	48	56	47
Canada	40	46	43	58	45
USA	—	—	—	—	21
Strongly support compulsory voting					
Australia	39	49	47	50	47
Great Britain	20	24	32	42	29
Canada	15	20	19	34	20

Question wording: Australia—"Do you think that voting at Federal elections should be compulsory, or do you think that people should only have to vote if they want to?" Canada—"In Australia, Belgium, Brazil, and a number of other countries, people are required by law to vote. How supportive would you be of a law like this for federal elections? Would you be very supportive, somewhat supportive, somewhat opposed, or very opposed?" Great Britain—"Which of these policies do you support or oppose? Make voting in elections compulsory." USA—"In a few countries every eligible citizen is required by law to vote in national elections. Those who don't have a good excuse for not voting are subject to a small fine. Do you think this would be a good law or a poor law to have in this country?"

Sources: 2004 Australian Election Study; 2001 MORI survey of Great Britain for the UK Electoral Commission; 2002, Elections Canada survey of Voters and Nonvoters; June 2004 ABC News Survey of USA (http://abcnews.go.com/images/pdf/883a44CompulsoryVoting.pdf) (accessed August 11, 2005).

60 percent in data compiled by Mackerras and McAllister dating back to 1943.[135] Interestingly, even young Australians clearly favor compulsory voting. At the same time, young respondents are also the least likely to say that they definitely would have voted had participation been voluntary.[136] Were it not for mandatory voting, there would be a significant age gap in electoral participation in Australia similar to that found in many other countries. The widespread support for compulsory voting among young

Australians indicates that they would rather not see their country slip into this pattern.

Whenever I talk to political science classes in Australia, I find that many of the students are amazed to learn how low turnout is for American elections. They immediately ask me why the United States doesn't just emulate their country's example and fine people who fail to participate. The best response I can think of is simply that most Americans object to the government telling them to do something, even if it is good for them. American political culture is based on John Locke's views of individual rights, which differ from Jeremy Bentham's concept of the greatest good for the greatest number, which shaped Australian culture. Most Americans would probably assert that they have an inviolable right not to show up at the polls. As former U.S. Attorney General Griffin Bell remarked during a brief discussion of compulsory voting at a 2001 hearing of the National Commission on Federal Election Reform, "That is not a free country when you are doing things like that."[137] While Griffin Bell's comment may be an extreme reaction, it is apparent from Table 9.2 that there has not been much support for requiring people to vote in the United States. Only 21 percent of Americans interviewed in a 2004 *ABC News* poll supported the idea of a compulsory voting law like that practiced in Australia.

As Table 9.2 shows, attitudes toward compulsory voting in Canada and Great Britain fall between the strong support for compulsory voting in Australia and the clear hostility to the idea in the United States. In both countries it is noteworthy that support for compulsory voting increases with age. Among senior citizens in Canada and Great Britain, a majority actually supports making voting mandatory. The high level of support for compulsory voting among older citizens can be explained by the facts that voters are substantially more likely than nonvoters to favor it and of course that older people have the highest turnout rates.

Citizens who vote apparently do not want to monopolize political power. Roughly half of voters in both Britain and Canada support the notion that participation by everyone is so important that the government should require it. If politicians listen primarily to those who vote, then they may well start to consider compulsory voting if turnout rates continue to fall, especially among young people. Indeed, a serious rumbling in this direction could be seen after turnout fell to a modern low in Britain. The former leader of the British House of Commons, Geoff Hoon, publicly stated that he thought a move to compulsory voting was necessary to reinvigorate UK democracy, arguing that "we need to get people more engaged in political processes."[138]

Most newsworthy of all was President Obama's positive mention of compulsory voting in response to a question in March 2015 about how to cure the "dysfunction" in Washington. Obama not only indicated that compulsory voting would be a good cure for what ails American politics but also specifically mentioned how this reform would bring more young people into the political system. His remarks on this subject are worth quoting at length:

> In Australia, and some other countries, there's mandatory voting. It would be transformative if everybody voted. That would counteract money more than anything. If everybody voted, then it would completely change the political map in this country, because the people who tend not to vote are young; they're lower income; they're skewed more heavily towards immigrant groups and minority groups; and they're often the folks who are—they're scratching and climbing to get into the middle class. And they're working hard, and there's a

reason why some folks try to keep them away from the polls.
We should want to get them into the polls. So that may end up
being a better strategy in the short term.[139]

When the president of the United States speaks out for the first time in favor of such a major change, it naturally attracts a lot of media attention, and this event was no exception. However, unlike most presidential statements, the idea of mandatory voting was rejected as far fetched by many commentators. As Fox News put it succinctly in a headline, "Constitution Experts on Obama Mandatory Voting Idea: Never Gonna Happen."[140]

I must confess my own initial reaction was not all that different from that of Fox News, as I viewed the president's statement as well intentioned but unrealistic. But after considering how the issue of gay marriage had evolved over the past two decades, it seemed to me that it was not so unrealistic after all. I realized that if President Clinton had proposed that gay couples should have a constitutional right to get married in 1996, most commentators would have scoffed that this would never happen. After all, at that point in history, the Congress had just overwhelmingly passed the Defense of Marriage Act, allowing states to refuse to recognize same-sex marriages granted elsewhere. By 2015, 37 states had already legalized gay marriage when the Supreme Court ruled this to be a constitutional right. In other words, what seems unrealistic at one point in time can become law within a generation.

Is Compulsory Voting at All Realistic?

When Arend Lijphart called for compulsory voting in his presidential address to the American Political Science Association, he wrote that "The danger of too much pessimism about the chances for compulsory voting is that it becomes a self-fulfilling prophecy. If even the supporters of compulsory voting believe that its chances are nil—and hence make no effort on behalf of it—it will indeed never be adopted!"[141] I wholeheartedly agree. Political scientists have been far too cautious in recommending compulsory voting despite what we know about the seriousness of the turnout problem among young people and how well this solution works to correct it.

Engineering safety experts have not backed off their recommendations calling for mandatory seat-belt laws for motorists just because many people think that whether to buckle up or not should be a matter of personal choice. Nor have researchers on secondhand smoke backed off on recommendations to ban smoking in public places just because many people think that such restrictions would be a violation of their individual rights. Rather, these researchers have continued to try to educate people and shift public policy, with the result being a fair degree of success. For example, in 2010 Gallup reported that 59 percent of the American public supported banning smoking in restaurants, up from a mere 17 percent in 1987.[142] As attitudes have changed, so have laws, with 38 U.S. states banning smoking in restaurants as of 2015. The campaign to increase the use of safety belts in automobiles has been equally impressive. Every state except New Hampshire now has a law requiring the use of seat belts.[143] Data compiled by the National Highway Traffic Safety Administration on actual usage of seat belts shows that the percentage of passengers using seat belts increased from 60 to 87 percent between 1995 and 2014.[144] In sum, attitudes and behavior can change as people become more aware of a problem; and once such changes are put into motion, politicians feel compelled to take actions that they never would have considered a decade or two earlier.

Ironically, one of the obstacles to the adoption of compulsory voting is the fear of success. Some analysts have trepidations about forcing people with limited political interest to appear at the polls. The fear is that, once compelled to vote, these citizens may make choices the same way some people choose lottery numbers. Or, worse yet, they may be particularly susceptible to demagogic appeals by irresponsible politicians with antidemocratic tendencies. Granted, these are serious concerns. But which is the worse scenario—a low and biased turnout with the participation of only those who follow politics, or a broad and representative turnout with the participation of people who follow politics as well as those who do not? Consider the situation in Italy as of 1959, when the Civic Culture Study found that about two-thirds of Italians said they *never* followed accounts of political and governmental affairs. Italy then had a compulsory voting law, and though it was not rigorously enforced, turnout nevertheless ranged between 92 and 95 percent. Looking back, can one really make a case that it would have been better if only the one-third of the Italian population who followed politics had voted?[145]

In his book *Culture War?*, Morris Fiorina writes that his students express outrage at the prospect of being forced to go to the polls even if they don't like any of the candidates.[146] My students, who are of course heavily exposed to the findings reviewed in this book, tend to be more outraged at the fact that older people are running the government while their generation is ignored due to its low turnout rate.

The answer to the question posed by the title of this book—*Is Voting for Young People?*—is that it certainly *should* be but all too often is not.

Endnotes

[1]Lara Jakes Jordan, "Harvard Rips Store's 'Old Voter' T-Shirt," Associated Press, March 1, 2004.

[2]See Doris Graber, *Mass Media and American Politics*, 6th ed. (Washington, DC: Congressional Quarterly Press, 2002).

[3]Colleen A. Sheehan, "Madison v. Hamilton: The Battle over Republicanism and the Role of Public Opinion," *American Political Science Review* 98 (2004): p. 421.

[4]See the September 23, 2003 interview transcript at http://www.foxnews.com/story/0,2933,98111,00.html (accessed February 7, 2004).

[5]See Helen Thomas, "No Wonder Bush Doesn't Connect with the Rest of the Country," Hearst Newspapers, October 15, 2003. See http://seattlepi.nwsource.com/opinion/143851_thomas15.html (accessed February 7, 2004).

[6]*Statistical Abstract of the United States*, 2002, p. 700.

[7]See Philip Meyer, *The Vanishing Newspaper: Saving Journalism in the Information Age* (Columbia: University of Missouri Press, 2004). Also see Frank Ahrens, "Hard News: Daily Papers Face Unprecedented Competition," *Washington Post*, February 20, 2005, p. F1.

[8]Cathy Scott-Clark and Adrian Levy, "Fast Forward into Trouble," *Guardian*, June 14, 2003.

[9]The justification for using this definition of regular newspaper reading is that the response options were judgment calls rather than specifics such as "every day." In my view, the major difference is between those who said "often" and "sometimes"—those who basically follow politics through a paper—and those who said "seldom" and "never"—those who basically do not. One person's sense of "often" might mean roughly half the time, while another person's sense of "sometimes" could be exactly the same. But it is hard to see how "seldom" could mean much more than once a week.

[10]Furthermore, the correlations found in the recent European data are probably underestimates because the variance in newspaper reading is truncated due to the poor choice of response categories offered. Most people who responded that they read a newspaper said they read it for less than 30 minutes. When asked the follow-up question of reading about politics, they had little choice but to say they read about politics for less than 30 minutes. There is no doubt a good deal of variation within this category, probably with younger readers spending less time with the newspaper than older ones, but the question's wording does not allow for this variance to be captured.

[11]The correlation between age and having read a book during the past year was –.11 in 1957 and –.04 in 2002. Controlling for education resulted in a partial correlation of –.04 in 1957 and .00 in 2002.

[12]John F. Kennedy, "A Force that Has Changed the Political Scene," *TV Guide*, November 14, 1959. This article can be found online at http://www.museum.tv/debateweb/html/equalizer/tvguide_jfkforce.htm (accessed January 7, 2005).

[13]Thomas E. Patterson and Robert D. McClure, *The Unseeing Eye: The Myth of Television Power in National Elections* (New York: Putnam, 1976), p. 58.

[14]See Paul F. Lazarsfeld, Bernard Berleson, and Hazel Gaudet, *The People's Choice* (New York: Columbia University Press, 1944).

[15]Shanto Iyengar and Donald R. Kinder, *News that Matters* (Chicago: University of Chicago Press, 1987).

[16]Ibid., pp. 118–119.

[17]Joanne M. Miller and Jon A. Krosnick, "News Media Impact on the Ingredients of Presidential Evaluations: Politically Knowledgeable Citizens Are Guided by a Trusted Source," *American Journal of Political Science*, 44 (April 2000): pp. 301–315.

[18]Jeff Alan, *Anchoring America: The Changing Face of Network News* (Chicago: Bonus Books, 2003), p. xiii.

[19]Barbara Matusow, *The Evening Stars: The Making of the Network News Anchor* (Boston: Houghton Mifflin, 1983), p. 1.

[20]Frank Rich, "The Weight of an Anchor," *New York Times*, May 19, 2002.

[21]The figure on the average age of the TV news audience can be found in "A Graying, Ailing Audience," *New York Times*, February 9, 2004, p. C6. The

figure for a typical prime-time show is cited in Robert D. Putnam, *Bowling Alone: The Collapse and Revival of American Community* (New York: Simon and Schuster, 2000), p. 221.

[22] Pew Research Center for the People and the Press, "Cable and Internet Loom Large in Fragmented Political News Universe," report released January 11, 2004, p. 10. This report can be found online at http://people-press.org/reports/pdf/200.pdf (accessed January 10, 2005).

[23] Ibid., p. 14.

[24] William Taubman and Jane Taubman, *Moscow Spring* (New York: Summit Books, 1989), p. 286.

[25] Project for Excellence in Journalism, *The State of the News Media, 2004*, posted at http://www.stateofthenewsmedia.org/index.asp (accessed August 27, 2004).

[26] Thomas Rosenstiel, "The End of Network News," *Washington Post*, September 12, 2004, p. B7.

[27] All responses of over 100 were recoded to 100. The correlation between age and the number of channels watched was 2.19.

[28] Byron E. Shafer, *Bifurcated Politics: Evolution and Reform in the National Party Convention* (Cambridge, MA: Harvard University Press, 1988), p. 274.

[29] Alan Schroeder, "There's No Debate About It: Face-to-Face, Candidates Let Their Masks Slip," *Washington Post*, October 17, 2004, p. B1. For a good history of these televised encounters, see Schroeder's book, *Presidential Debates: Forty Years of High-Risk TV* (New York: Columbia University Press, 2000).

[30] In 2004, the average presidential debate rating was 33, reflecting the greater interest in this campaign.

[31] Marshall McLuhan, *Understanding Media* (New York: McGraw-Hill, 1964).

[32] Edward J. Epstein, *News from Nowhere: Television and the News* (New York: Random House, 1973).

[33] Ibid., p. 17.

[34] The sample frame included all people at least 16 years of age. The age question did not ask for each respondent's exact age, but rather for an age range. Because the age range was 16 to 20 years of age, one either has to exclude 18-, 19-, and

20-year-olds or include the 16- and 17-year-olds. I thought it better to include some respondents who were not quite of voting age rather than exclude some respondents who could vote.

[35]The R squared value, measuring the degree to which one variable explains variance in another, increased from .012 in 1970 to .064 in 2000.

[36]An analysis of European Social Survey data from 2002–2003 adds further confidence to this estimate. This survey asked Europeans, "On an average weekday, how much time, in total, do you spend watching television? And again on an average weekday, how much of your time watching television is spent watching *news* or programmes about *politics and current affairs?*" The average correlation between age and the number of minutes spent watching news about politics was .29 in the 12 established democracies other than Italy (which once again was found to be an outlying case).

[37]In spite of winning these debates, both John Turner in Canada and Mark Latham in Australia saw their respective parties lose the election. As John Kerry found out in the United States, success in televised debates is no guarantee of victory at the polls.

[38]Australian Associated Press, "*Australian Idol* Beats Election Debate," September 13, 2004.

[39]James T. Hamilton, *All the News That's Fit to Sell* (Princeton, NJ: Princeton University Press, 2004), p. 7.

[40]Ibid., p. 70.

[41]Matthew A. Baum, *Soft News Goes to War: Public Opinion and American Foreign Policy in the New Media Age* (Princeton, NJ: Princeton University Press, 2003), p. 7.

[42]David T. Z. Mindich, *Tuned Out: Why Americans Under 40 Don't Follow the News* (New York: Oxford University Press, 2005), p. 39.

[43]Ibid., p. 40.

[44]See Norman Nie, Jane Junn, and Kenneth Stehlik-Barry, *Education and Democratic Citizenship in America* (Chicago: University of Chicago Press, 1996), pp. 114–118.

[45]See Michael X. Delli Carpini and Scott Keeter, *What Americans Know About Politics and Why It Matters* (New Haven, CT: Yale University Press, 1996),

pp. 196–199. In their detailed analysis over time, Delli Carpini and Keeter also conclude that the relative impact of education on political knowledge has been fairly constant over the past half century.

[46]Gabriel A. Almond and Sidney Verba, *The Civic Culture* (Boston: Little, Brown, and Co., 1963), pp. 206–207.

[47]Ibid., p. 308.

[48]Ibid., p. 57.

[49]I initially created two separate indices—one for the number of Common Market countries named and the other for recall of the two political leaders. The results by age were almost identical for these two indices, and therefore I have combined them to simplify the presentation.

[50]The data on knowledge of who won *American Idol* and *The Simpsons'* hometown can be found in Karl T. Kurtz, Alan Rosenthal, and Cliff Zukin, "Citizenship: A Challenge for All Generations," report of the National Conference of State Legislatures, September 2003. This report can be found at http://www.cpn.org/topics/youth/k12/pdfs/NCSL_Citizenship.pdf (accessed March 4, 2005). The data on the Super Bowl winner is from Harvard's 2000 "Vanishing Voter" project.

[51]Stephen Earl Bennett and Eric W. Rademacher, "The Age of Indifference Revisited: Patterns of Political Interest, Media Exposure, and Knowledge Among Generation X," in *After the Boom: The Politics of Generation X*, ed. Stephen C. Craig and Stephen Earl Bennett (Lanham, MD: Rowman and Littlefield, 1997), p. 39.

[52]Delli Carpini and Keeter, *What Americans Know*, chap. 6.

[53]Of course, political scientists have come up with many reasons for why people vote. For a review of the factors that influence who votes, see Raymond E. Wolfinger and Steven J. Rosenstone, *Who Votes?* (New Haven, CT: Yale University Press, 1980) and Martin P. Wattenberg, *Where Have All the Voters Gone?* (Cambridge, MA: Harvard University Press, 2002), chap. 3.

[54]See U.S. Bureau of the Census, *Current Population Reports*, Series P-20, No. 143, "Voter Participation in the National Election: November 1964" (Washington, DC: U.S. Government Printing Office, 1965), p. 1. This report can be found at http://www.census.gov/population/www/socdemo/voting/p20–143.html (accessed June 11, 2005).

[55]President's Commission on Registration and Voting Participation, "Report on Registration and Voting Participation" (Washington, DC: U.S. Government Printing Office, 1963), p. 43.

[56]Jane Eisner, *Taking Back the Vote: Getting American Youth Involved in Our Democracy* (Boston: Beacon Press, 2004), p. 3.

[57]Alexander Keyssar, *The Right to Vote: The Contested History of Democracy in the United States* (New York: Basic Books, 2000), p. 281.

[58]Quoted in Eisner, *Taking Back the Vote*, p. 31.

[59]Benjamin Highton and Raymond E. Wolfinger, "The First Seven Years of the Political Life Cycle," *American Journal of Political Science* 45 (2001): pp. 202–209.

[60]The information for these age categories can be found at http://www.census. gov/population/www/socdemo/voting.html (accessed June 21, 2005).

[61]Following the framework outlined in Russell J. Dalton and Martin P. Wattenberg, eds., *Parties Without Partisans* (Oxford: Oxford University Press, 2001), p. 14, I have limited the sample of countries to those that 1) have been democracies continuously since World War II, 2) belong to the OECD, and 3) have substantial population size (thereby excluding Iceland and Luxembourg).
   Whenever possible, I have used data from national election studies, choosing the time point closest to November 1972. For countries that had no election studies available—Finland, Austria, and Italy—I used data from the Political Action Study that asked respondents whether they had voted in the most recent national election.

[62]On this question in Denmark, see Jorgen Elklit, Palle Svensson, and Lise Togeby, "Why Is Voter Turnout Not Declining in Denmark?," paper presented at the 2005 meeting of the American Political Science Association.

[63]Mark N. Franklin, *Voter Turnout and the Dynamics of Electoral Competition in Established Democracies Since 1945* (New York: Cambridge University Press, 2004), p. 206.

[64]The legal specification is actually more complex. The National Voter Registration Act of 1993 states that removal can occur only if someone "has not voted or appeared to vote (and, if necessary, correct the registrar's record of the registrant's address) in an election during the period beginning on the date of the notice and ending on the day after the date of the second general election for Federal office that occurs after the date of the notice." In practice, this amounts to roughly four years before someone can be purged.

[65] Alan Ware, *The Breakdown of Democratic Party Organization, 1940–1980* (New York: Oxford University Press, 1985), p. 203.

[66] I am indebted to Mark Gray for obtaining and processing these data and making them available to me.

[67] Voting in local government elections is compulsory in some Australian states, and it is interesting to note the differences in voter turnout rates in such elections. In New South Wales and Queensland, for example, where voting is compulsory, turnout rates have been more than 85 percent in non-Federal elections. But in other states, where voting in local government elections is not compulsory, turnout rates have been much lower. For example, only about 58 percent of enrolled people voted in Tasmania's 2002 local election, and only 38 percent voted in Western Australia's May 2001 local election.

[68] In 2001 the Western Australian Electoral Commission found nearly identical results by age.

[69] See the October/November 2002 Eurobarometer. Thirty-six percent said this statement was false, and 21 percent said they did not know.

[70] The turnout figures for each country from 1979 to 2004 can be found at http://www.elections2004.eu.int/ep-election/sites/en/results1306/turnout_ep/turnout_table.html (accessed July 5, 2005).

[71] Subsequent data from the 2004 and 2009 European Election Studies continue to bolster this point.

[72] Franklin, *Voter Turnout*, p. 213.

[73] Interestingly, Mark Franklin writes favorably about this idea, arguing that this probably would work better than the current voting age of 18 practiced in most countries. See note 72.

[74] In most national surveys, there would not be sufficient cases to do such an analysis with such narrowly defined age groups. The fact that the European Social Survey was conducted in numerous countries makes it possible to aggregate more than enough cases to get a reliable reading on the media habits of 16-to-17-year-olds.

[75] Angus Campbell, Philip E. Converse, Warren E. Miller, and Donald E. Stokes, *The American Voter* (Chicago: University of Chicago Press, 1960), p. 105.

[76] Andre Blais, *To Vote or Not to Vote* (Pittsburgh: University of Pittsburgh Press, 2000), p. 92.

[77] I first went on a scouting trip to see if there was a wheelchair at the polling place, without which I figured it would be next to impossible for my father to vote. There indeed was one, but I noticed there was a lot of competition for access to it. When I reported back to my parents that they might have to wait a while for my father to get use of the wheelchair, they said this was all right. We proceeded to the polling place, and all went well. It was while waiting for my parents to vote that I observed that the average age of people voting in this midterm election was quite high, and the idea for this book was first hatched in my mind.

[78] Two percent picked all, 1 percent said none, and 2 percent said they didn't know.

[79] Blais, *To Vote or Not to Vote*, p. 97.

[80] M. Kent Jennings and Richard G. Niemi, *The Political Character of Adolescence: The Influence of Families and Schools* (Princeton, NJ: Princeton University Press, 1974), p. 122.

[81] M. Kent Jennings and Richard G. Niemi, *Generations and Politics: A Panel Study of Young Adults and Their Parents* (Princeton, NJ: Princeton University Press, 1981), p. 125.

[82] In 1997, data were also gathered from a sample of the children of the class of 1965. However, as this third-generation sample was contacted only by mail, they were not asked the open-ended question concerning the qualities of a good citizen.

[83] Wolfinger and Rosenstone, *Who Votes?*, p. 111.

[84] Ruy A. Teixeira, *The Disappearing American Voter* (Washington, DC: The Brookings Institution, 1992), p. 95.

[85] Sidney Verba, Kay Lehman Schlozman, and Henry E. Brady, *Voice and Equality: Civic Voluntarism in American Politics* (Cambridge, MA: Harvard University Press, 1995), p. 205.

[86] David R. Mayhew, *Congress: The Electoral Connection* (New Haven, CT: Yale University Press, 1974).

[87] John W. Kingdon, *Agendas, Alternatives, and Public Policies*, 2nd ed. (New York: HarperCollins, 1995).

[88] Other data collections, such as the American National Election Studies, the Pew Research Center surveys, and the National Annenberg Election Study, confirm this pattern.

[89]Because nonvoters tend to be less conservative than voters, it is hard to see how they would have voted more for Bush. Thus, making this assumption probably involves slightly underestimating just how much equalizing the turnout rate among ages would have swung the vote in Gore's favor.

[90]See Russell J. Dalton, *Citizen Politics: Public Opinion and Political Parties in Advanced Industrial Democracies*, 3rd ed. (Chatham, NJ: Chatham House, 2002).

[91]Excluding the countries that practice compulsory voting—Australia and Belgium—increases the correlation to .80.

[92]I am indebted to Aiji Tanaka of Waseda University for sharing his 2003 survey data with me for this purpose.

[93]Editorial, *Asahi Shimbun*, November 3, 2003.

[94]Jane Eisner, *Taking Back the Vote: Getting American Youth Involved in Our Democracy* (Boston: Beacon Press, 2004), p. 54.

[95]Cliff Zukin, Scott Keeter, Molly Andolina, Krista Jenkins, and Michael X. Delli Carpini, *A New Engagement? Political Participation, Civic Life, and the Changing American Citizen* (New York: Oxford University Press, 2006), p. 3.

[96]Ibid., p. 7.

[97]Russell J. Dalton, "Citizenship Norms and Political Participation in America: The Good News Is ... The Bad News Is Wrong," paper presented at the conference on Citizens, Involvement and Democracy, Georgetown University, December 2005, p. 9.

[98]Ibid., pp. 13–14.

[99]Ibid., p. 9.

[100]Ganesh Sitaraman and Previn Warren, *Invisible Citizens: Youth Politics After September 11* (New York: iUniverse, Inc., 2003), p. ix.

[101]Stephen Macedo et al., *Democracy at Risk: How Political Choices Undermine Citizen Participation, and What We Can Do About It* (Washington, DC: Brookings Institution, 2005), p. 123.

[102]Sitaraman and Warren, *Invisible Citizens*, p. 17.

[103]Macedo et al., *Democracy at Risk*, p. 125.

[104]Zukin et al., *A New Engagement?*, pp. 193–200.

[105]Samuel H. Barnes and Max Kaase, *Political Action: Mass Participation in Five Western Democracies* (Beverly Hills: Sage, 1979), p. 524.

[106]Andrea Louise Campbell, *How Policies Make Citizens: Senior Political Activism and the American Welfare State* (Princeton, NJ: Princeton University Press, 2003), p. 15.

[107]David Von Drehle, "The Year of the Youth Vote," *Time*, January 31, 2008. See http://www.time.com/time/politics/article/0,8599,1708570-2,00.html (accessed October 1, 2015).

[108]Jamilah King, Kristina Rizga, and Tomas Palermo, "Election Victory: Yes We Did!," *Wiretap*, December 27, 2008.

[109]See http://people-press.org/report/467/internet-campaign-news (accessed October 1, 2015).

[110]Matthew Hindman, *The Myth of Digital Democracy* (Princeton, NJ: Princeton University Press, 2009).

[111]Ibid., p. 68.

[112]See http://www.naa.org/Trends-and-Numbers/Newspaper-Revenue/ Newspaper-Media-Industry-Revenue-Profile-2013.aspx (accessed October 1, 2015).

[113]See Cecilia Kang, "TV Is Increasingly for Old People," *Washington Post*, September 5, 2014.

[114]Steve Sternberg, "The Median Age Report," *Media Insights*, June 30, 2008. See http://tvbythenumbers.com/wp-content/uploads/2008/06/2008-median-age-report.pdf (accessed October 1, 2015).

[115]Markus Prior, *Post-Broadcast Democracy* (New York: Cambridge University Press, 2007), p. 133.

[116]Ibid., p. 266.

[117]Ibid., p. 248

[118]Data on the reliance on demographics of phone usage can be found at http://www.cdc.gov/nchs/data/nhis/earlyrelease/wireless201412.pdf (accessed October 1, 2015).

[119]Michael McDonald, "The True Electorate: A Cross-Validation of Voter Registration Files and Election Survey Demographics," *Public Opinion Quarterly* (Winter 2007): p.600.

[120]The exit polls reported that 18 percent of Democratic primary voters and 11 percent of Republican primary voters were under the age of 30. Given the total Democratic turnout of 1,056,251 and the total Republican turnout of 958,293, it can be estimated that the total number of young voters based on the exit polls was 295,537. For senior citizens, the exit polls reported that 11 percent were under 30 and 16 percent were senior citizens, thereby producing an estimate of 258,951 seniors at the polls. These estimates of the actual number voting can then be divided by the Census Bureau's estimates of the 2008 population—1,635,530 under the age of 30 and 981,024 for senior citizens—to produce the turnout percentages reported in the text.

In contrast, the actual records showed that 203,093 ballots were cast by voters under the age of 30 and 395,723 ballots were cast by voters above 65 years of age. Again, dividing by the Census Bureau's population estimates produces the relevant turnout percentages.

[121]If one factors in the lower likelihood of being registered to vote among younger citizens, the generational gap in primary turnout would be even greater.

[122]Sam Stein, "Obama to Young Voters: 'You Can't Sit Out' in 2010," *Huffington Post*, September 27, 2010. See http://www.huffingtonpost.com/2010/09/27/obama-to-young-voters-you_n_740442.html (accessed October 1, 2015).

[123]The California Civic Engagement Project's report on turnout in 2014 can be found online at http://explore.regionalchange.ucdavis.edu/ourwork/projects/copy2_of_UCDavisCCEPPolicyBrief92014YouthVote.pdf (accessed October 1, 2015).

[124]See Celeste Katz, "Ahead of NYC Special Elections, New Report a Reminder that Voter Turnout Stinks," *New York Daily News*, May 1, 2015. See http://www.nydailynews.com/blogs/dailypolitics/nyc-voter-turnout-stinks-blog-entry-1.2207074 (accessed October 1, 2015).

[125]Arend Lijphart, "Unequal Participation: Democracy's Unresolved Dilemma," *American Political Science Review* 91 (1997): p. 10.

[126]Richard G. Niemi and Jane Junn, *Civic Education: What Makes Students Learn* (New Haven, CT: Yale University Press, 1998).

[127]In the 1972 Census Bureau survey, citizenship status was not ascertained. Among all people aged 18 to 24, the registration rate in 1972 was 59 percent. It is my best estimate, based on the relatively small percentage of noncitizens then living in the United States, that roughly 61 percent of 18- to 24-year-old citizens were registered to vote. In any event, it is unquestionable that the percentage of young citizens who are registered to vote declined between 1972 and 2012, despite the easing of registration procedures.

[128]Thomas E. Patterson, *The Vanishing Voter* (New York: Knopf, 2002). See p. 182 for a list of Patterson's policy proposals.

[129]Ibid., p. 149.

[130]The question wording was as follows: "Some people say the presidential campaign is so long that they don't have time to pay attention except now and then. Other people say they like the long presidential campaign because it gives them a better chance to get to know the candidates. Which view is closer to your own? Do you think the campaign is too long or do you prefer a long campaign?" This question was asked in six different weekly surveys, and was answered by a total of 2,255 respondents.

[131]For example, in 2002, the U.S. Census Bureau found that 30 percent of registered nonvoters aged 18 to 24 said they were too busy to vote on election day, whereas only 5 percent of senior citizens who were registered and did not vote chose this excuse.

[132]Jack Vowles, "Offsetting the PR Effect? Party Mobilization and Turnout Decline in New Zealand, 1996–99," *Party Politics* 8 (2002): pp. 587–605.

[133]In Australia the typical fine for nonvoting is 20 Australian dollars. However, judges typically accept any reasonable excuse, and few people end up paying a fine for not voting. In the Australian Federal election of 2004, there were about 13 million enrolled voters, 94.3 percent of whom participated. Of the approximately 740,000 nonvoters, only about 50,000 actually paid a fine. In Belgium, the percentage of nonvoters who pay a fine is even smaller, as the Minister of Justice has declared enforcement of compulsory voting fines a low priority. Nevertheless, turnout in Belgium has remained extremely high.

[134]Lijphart, "Unequal Participation," p. 2.

[135] Malcolm Mackerras and Ian McAllister, "Compulsory Voting, Party Stability, and Electoral Advantage in Australia," *Electoral Studies* 18 (1999): p. 221.

[136] Fifty-four percent of people between the ages of 18 and 29 said they would definitely have voted in 2004 had voting been voluntary, compared to 77 percent among Australian senior citizens.

[137] Judge Griffin Bell, National Commission on Federal Election Reform, Public Hearing 1, Panel IV, transcript, p. 13.

[138] "Hoon Suggests Compulsory Voting," *BBC News World Edition*, July 4, 2005.

[139] "Remarks by the President to the City Club of Cleveland," March 18, 2015. The entire speech and question-and-answer session can be found at https://www.whitehouse.gov/the-press-office/2015/03/18/remarks-president-city-club-cleveland (accessed October 1, 2015).

[140] Cristina Corbin, "Constitution Experts on Obama Mandatory Voting Idea: Never Gonna Happen," March 20, 2015. See http://www.foxnews.com/politics/2015/03/20/mandatory-voting-experts/ (accessed October 1, 2015).

[141] Lijphart, "Unequal Participation," p. 11.

[142] *Lydia Saad*, "Americans Want Smoking off the Menu at Restaurants," Gallup Poll report, August 6, 2010.

[143] As of 2015, 34 states had primary-enforcement laws, meaning that motorists can be given a ticket for no reason other than simply not fastening their seat belt. Fifteen other states had secondary-enforcement laws, whereby drivers must be stopped for another violation before being given a citation for not using a seat belt.

[144] T. M. Pickrell and E. H. Choi, "Safety Belt Use in 2014—Overall Results," Traffic Safety Facts Research Note, February 2015, National Highway Traffic Safety Administration. This study found that 91 percent of passengers were buckled up in 2005 in states with primary-enforcement laws, compared to 80 percent in states with secondary-enforcement laws.

[145] Lest one think that an established democracy could never see such low turnout for a national election, I'd point out that turnout rates for U.S. midterm congressional elections have regularly been between 33 and 40 percent in recent decades.

[146] Morris P. Fiorina (with Samuel J. Abrams and Jeremy C. Pope), *Culture War?* (New York: Longman, 2005), p. 111.

Index

Name Index

Subject Index